WEED FREE GARDENING

Inspiring | Educating | Creating | Entertaining

Brimming with creative inspiration, how-to projects, and useful information to enrich your everyday life, quarto.com is a favorite destination for those pursuing their interests and passions.

26 25 24 23 22   1 2 3 4 5

ISBN: 978-0-7603-7323-1

Digital edition published in 2022
eISBN: 978-0-7603-7324-8

Library of Congress Cataloging-in-Publication Data
Names: Greer, Tasha, author.
Title: Weed-free gardening : a comprehensive and organic approach to weed management / Tasha Greer.
Other titles: Comprehensive and organic approach to weed management
Description: Beverly : Cool Springs Press, 2022. | Includes bibliography and index. | Summary: "Weed-Free Gardening introduces a comprehensive and achievable plan for eliminating weed pressure in your planting beds"-- Provided by publisher.
Identifiers: LCCN 2021047023 | ISBN 9780760373231 (trade paperback) | ISBN 9780760373248 (ebook)
Subjects: LCSH: Weeds--Control--Handbooks, manuals, etc. | Weeds--Biological control--Handbooks, manuals, etc. | Organic gardening--Weed control.
Classification: LCC SB611.5 .G73 2022 | DDC 632/.5--dc23/eng/20211001
LC record available at https://lccn.loc.gov/2021047023

Design & Page Layout: Tanya Jacobson
Photography (Reference: T=Top, B=Bottom): All photos Tasha Poulain except for Alamy: 28-29, Ashlie Thomas: 139T, 139B, Misilla Dela Llana: 138T, 138B, Niki Jabbour: 140, 141, Shutterstock: 4, 14, 16, 18, 19, 57T, 78, 88T, 95, 96, 108-109, 114, 115, 129T, 132-133, 147, 150-151, 170-171, 178-179
Illustration: Greta Moore

Printed in China

WEED
FREE
GARDENING

A Comprehensive and
——————— Organic Approach ———————
to Weed Management

TASHA GREER

author of
Grow Your Own Spices

COOL
SPRINGS
PRESS

INTRODUCTION

The War on Weeds, Why It Can't Be Won, and How to Make Peace in the Garden

PART ONE

WEED PREVENTION

PART TWO

MAINTENANCE

PART THREE

RECONCILIATION

PART FOUR

CREATING PEACE IN THE GARDEN

This is an example of interplanting for weed prevention. Sorghum, amaranth, and sunflowers provide vertical structure. Job's tears (*Coix lacryma-jobi*) and Maypop passion flowers vine up. Pumpkin leaves give weed cover. Cherry tomatoes, jalapeños, and basil ensure I come to harvest and do minor weed control on the patch.

INTRODUCTION

The War on Weeds, Why It Can't Be Won, and How to Make Peace in the Garden

Getting into the Weeds

There is no single, magic answer to make weeds go away safely. It takes a selection of targeted strategies and regular garden maintenance to stay ahead of potential plant invaders. Yet, there are many ways to make weeding easier and more enjoyable while also improving your soil, growing healthier plants, and enhancing the beauty of your landscape and garden.

In this book, I'll share an arsenal of broad-spectrum weed control tools, tricks, and practices that don't require chemical warfare. We'll also get into fun ways to integrate popular weed-free methods, such as square foot, straw bale, no dig, grow bag, and raised bed gardening throughout your landscape. We'll even touch on weeds in the context of comprehensive gardening systems, such as permaculture and ecological restoration.

The information in these pages will also free you from the modern cultural aversion to plants that grow on their own. While it is true that there are some "true weeds" that must be controlled, most self-sowing or easily spreading plants don't deserve to be treated like weeds at all. These helpful volunteers can improve our gardening practices, make our landscapes healthier, and may have edible or medicinal value.

Are mugwort (*Artemisia vulgaris*) and henbit (*Lamium amplexicaule*) weeds or easy-to-grow edible and medicinal plants that help crowd out other weeds? Before you decide, do a little research to see if this information changes how you perceive these plants.

Finally, I understand the lure of those sublime weed-free gardens seen on social media, in magazines, and in books. Even when we know that it took a team of gardeners, a professional photographer, and artful manipulation to capture that moment of perfection, we still cling to those unattainable standards of beauty at home. So, as part of a comprehensive weed management approach, I will help reset your aesthetic expectations for what truly beautiful gardens look like. Toward that end, I'll expose the weed secrets of some renowned gardeners.

We'll study up on five key types of weed-like plants that may need controlling and learn about our human history of weeding. Then, the rest of the book is broken down into four parts: prevention, maintenance, reconciliation, and creating peace in the garden. As we work our way through the book, you'll see these sections interrelate to form a whole picture of restorative gardening.

In all things gardening, an ounce of prevention is better than a pound of cure, as the saying goes. So, Part 1 focuses on understanding weeds in order to take strategic action. Of course, even with good prevention methods, you'll still need to do regular maintenance on your garden to keep weeds away. Part 2 goes through ways to keep improving your garden conditions. Part 3 is directed at improving our relationship with so-called invader plants. Finally, Part 4 is where we get into the garden together. There you'll find inspiration and easy ways to help you end your war on weeds and enjoy peace in your garden.

In many gardens, violets are a nature-provided soil protector. A few leaves of false strawberry and curly dock are also in this mix, ready to take over when the violets time out in warmer weather.

What Is a Weed?

"A weed is a plant out of place." This is an awesome way to describe many volunteer plants that show up uninvited in our landscapes. For this book, though, I'll specifically address five types of weed-like plants.

LET'S GET INTO THE WEEDS!

WEED TYPE 1

PLANTS ADAPTED TO PROTECT EXPOSED SOIL AFTER NATURAL DISASTERS

In nature, there are no weeds, only plants that solve problems or fill niches in an ecosystem. For example, imagine the natural cycle that unfolds after a forest fire.

Deadnettle (*Lamium purpureum*) is easy to remove if you lift the leaves and pull by the crown. It's also a wonderful cool season ground cover that limits the spread of other weeds, such as the Carolina geranium lurking here.

Without the tree canopy and leaf litter to shade the soil, previously dormant seeds, exposed to light, suddenly germinate. These plants grow, flower, produce more seeds, and quickly die. Within a year or two, several generations of volunteer plants have grown and died back, making natural mulch over the burned area. Underground, decaying roots protect topsoil and feed rebounding populations of soil life.

As the soil stabilizes in response to being protected, plants from adjacent forest areas send runners into the burn zone to start new plants. Nearby trees and shrubs drop seeds that roll into the area, germinate, and take root in the moist mulch. These plants grow and shade the soil, preventing those fast-growing, self-sowing plant seeds from germinating. Soon, the slower growing forest plants dominate again.

In our gardens, we often disturb our land much like a fire would. By eliminating native vegetation—raking out leaf litter, digging into the subsoil to remove unwanted plants, and allowing topsoil to erode by wind and rain—our actions trigger weeds to spring into action to protect soil.

But these plants aren't weeds. They're heroes! For example, prolific cool weather weeds like chickweed (*Stellaria media*), deadnettle (*Lamium purpureum*), violet (*Viola sororia*), ground ivy (*Glechoma hederacea* syn. *Nepeta glechoma* Benth., *Nepeta hederacea*) protect bare soil when gardeners and other plants take their winter break. You can also easily control these weeds by cutting back their leaf matter for the compost pile, then covering them with a few layers of paper and mulch.

Spiny amaranth (*Amaranthus spinosus*) has lovely flowers and prolific edible seeds. Beware of the barbed stems. Also, expect them to cross-pollinate with cultivated amaranths in your flower garden.

WEED TYPE 2

PLANTS ADAPTED TO TAKE ADVANTAGE OF OUR AGRICULTURAL PRACTICES

There are more insidious characters that have evolved specifically in response to our agricultural methods. These plants come in all forms—perennials, annuals, taproot, fibrous-root, ground cover, shrubbery, and trees. They reproduce rapidly, thrive in disturbed soil, and grow better than cultivated plants in poor conditions (e.g., droughts, floods, and soil nutrient imbalances).

They've also evolved mechanisms for spreading over long distances, including exploding seed pods, sticky seeds, aerodynamic seed dispersal systems, moving across and under land (with rhizomes, runners/stolons), and reproducing from root or stem pieces. For example, the dandelion (*Taraxacum officinale*) seed heads plucked by children and blown to make a wish were designed by nature to spread by wind over long distances.

Many of these so-called weeds got their start as farmed and foraged plants. They grow everywhere because they migrate with humans. Lawn weeds like clovers and sprawling grasses were transported across oceans as livestock fodder. Spiny amaranth (*Amaranthus spinosus*), an American export, was grown for its edible seeds and stems. Today, this pretty and palatable plant's habit of cross-pollinating decorative amaranths and barbed stems make it a garden menace.

Unfortunately, as former cultivated plants, this class of weeds knows our ways and grows well even though we no longer want them to. Ralph Waldo Emerson's famously wrote, "What is a weed? A plant whose virtues have not yet been discovered." But in fact, many weeds are plants whose virtues have been forgotten. For this type of weeds, once you know their histories and uses, you may decide to reconcile your differences and coexist compatibly in your landscape.

The American elderberry (*Sambucus canadensis*), native to North America, grows in a broad range of soil types and suckers and self-sows easily. Its edible lacelike flower heads, purple medicinal berries, and speckled multi-trunk are lovely in an edible landscape.

WEED TYPE 3

CULTIVATED OR NATIVE PLANTS THAT BEHAVE LIKE WEEDS

Cultivated or native plants that grow quickly, expand their territory by multiple propagation methods, and require management to contain are also sometimes mistakenly classed as weeds. Goldenrod, strawberries, culinary mint, horseradish, bamboo, and elderberry are a few examples that come to mind from my garden.

These kinds of plants aren't true weeds, they're just productive in tough conditions. Yet, once you learn the secrets to growing them responsibly, you'll stop seeing them as invasive and begin to see them as the beautiful garden allies they truly are.

• Goldenrod (*Solidago*) self-seeds so readily it can fill a meadow or a poorly managed garden in no time. Thankfully, its seeds require light to germinate. That makes mulching an effective tool for control.

• Strawberry plants simply want to be shared with all your gardening friends.

• Cut and dried mint leaves make a perfect mulch, livestock litter additive, or compost additive.

• Horseradish roots love a container or to become homemade horseradish sauce.

• Bamboo shoots are delicious when eaten in spring before they spread.

• Homemade elderflower cordials and elderberry wine make this plant perfect for edible landscapes if grown on raised mounds or in heavy, wet soil to slow suckering.

Shifts in perspective and finding uses for these eager, productive plants can prevent them from becoming weeds in your garden.

WEED TYPE 4

PLANTS DETRIMENTAL TO ECOSYSTEMS OR HUMAN ENTERPRISES

These two young trees-of-heaven (*Ailanthus altissima*) insinuating themselves between the tulip poplar and maple require mowing and shallow root removal. Established stands take significantly more work to control.

Now we come to plants that genuinely deserve the term weed. These are often invasive in the legal sense— classified as such by our governments for the common good. They start out as imported ornamentals or arrive accidentally in imported plants, seed packets, or agricultural products.

Without their native pests and diseases to impede their growth, and in amenable climate or soil conditions, they spread quickly. They can pose threats to native species, to wildlife, and to agriculture. Their excessive growth, ability to host new pests and pathogens, and resistance to certain weed control methods can threaten infrastructure and human health. For example, the tree-of-heaven (*Ailanthus altissima*) is an escaped ornamental threatening my region.

It's a stunning leguminous tree that fixes nitrogen, grows quickly even in shade, and spreads by underground runners. Its decaying leaves have allelopathic properties that suppress the growth of nearby plants, making it a fearsome foe for native plant populations. Plus, it's the preferred host plant of the imported spotted lanternfly. That leafhopper, known for decimating vineyards, is following the trail of invasive tree-of-heaven down the American East Coast and wreaking havoc on viticultural regions.

These invasive plants put ecosystems, agriculture, and people's livelihoods at risk. We have a civic duty to eradicate them in our landscapes. Unfortunately, these are the most difficult to control. Expect to do some work to control them. Also, keep an updated invasive plant list for your bioregion handy. Be on the lookout to control new invaders early. Your closest agricultural education office or regional invasive plant council can provide you with current information.

Forested areas clear-cut for human development, such as for housing, pasture, or gardens, will quickly regrow if returning vegetation isn't managed like invading weeds.

WEED TYPE 5

VEGETATION CLEARED FOR GARDENING OR AGRICULTURE

The way we think about weeds today—as garden or agricultural invaders in need of killing—is a recent development that only came about starting in the 1950s when synthetic herbicides made their agricultural debut. Before that, for most of our 200,000-year human history, we were nomadic hunters and gatherers reliant on wild plants and game as resources. In that context, the idea of weeds wouldn't have existed. Then, about 12,000 years ago, humans around the world began to farm.

To grow crops and create human settlements, existing trees and vegetation had to be cleared. Initially, this was done with slash-and-burn techniques. Primitive

hand tools, such as digging sticks and stone hoes, were also used. The act of clearing land for farming and housing was the start of when humans began treating wild plants as weeds.

Today, to clear large areas of existing vegetation you'll likely need special excavation equipment or approval from the fire department for a controlled burn. So, I won't cover that in a gardening book. However, as early farmers discovered and modern gardeners know well, clearing the land is only a temporary fix. Eventually, that native or naturalized vegetation will return. This book can help.

Of course, the plants that come back aren't really weeds. They're just residents trying to rebuild. Yet, to prevent them from re-occupying territory, you'll have to pretend like those plants are weeds for several years.

Today tractors are used to apply herbicides, plow, and sow seeds in straight rows, as well as hoe and spray weeds between rows after planting.

A Short History of Weed Control Methods

Now that we've clarified the five types of weeds this book will help you manage, let's take a brief look at our history of weed management to better understand why we must take a new approach to weed control going forward.

As mentioned earlier, slash-and-burn and digging sticks and stone hoes were the primary weed control tools until about 5,800 years ago. Then a proto-plow called an "ard" left historically traceable marks in ancient soil. It was a simple wooden tool pulled by cattle used to uproot existing vegetation.

Roughly 4,000 years ago, Egyptian pharaohs began creating pleasure gardens intended to go with them to the afterlife. Raised beds, hardscaping, and (sadly) slave labor were likely the main weed control methods employed in those elaborate gardens.

About 2,600 years ago, straight row cropping of a single crop type became common. That innovation allowed farmers to mow and hoe between rows after planting. This made harvesting easier, but it also necessitated more weeding in bare soil between rows. In many cultures, this was done by children or slaves.

By the height of the Roman Empire, sophisticated plows with metal blades were extensively used. During the Third Punic War, Romans even plowed salt—the first natural broad-spectrum herbicide—into the Carthaginians' crop fields to starve survivors. Ironically, many historians attribute the fall of Rome to the decline of soil health in the Roman heartland caused by excessive plowing.

Around 900 years ago, Aztecs farmed on chinampas or mounded beds surrounded by canals of fresh water. They may have dumped feces into the canals, where it combined with the water and soil runoff to make "night soil." Farmers dug out and applied the mixture on top of leaves around the planting holes. This fertilized and controlled weeds. (We still use something like night soil under the name "biosolids" on farm fields and home lawns.)

Interplanting of different species to reduce weeds, increase yields, and diversify the diet was also common in Aztec and other cultures. For example, maize (corn) was planted with beans and squash in a practice that is now referred to as the "three sisters." The ground-vining squash provided shade cover to suppress the germination of weeds. The corn stalks provided trellising for the beans to make harvesting easier.

It's important to note that even though humans farmed, they also still hunted and foraged to round out their caloric and medicinal needs. Until supermarkets and the Green Revolution made food more affordable in the 1950s, foraging was common even in industrialized countries. Until about seventy years ago many of the plants we call weeds today were continuously valued as free food, medicine, livestock fodder, and kindling, or used in crafts.

In World War II in the United States, under a military secrecy act, herbicide research was conducted to create chemical weapons intended to kill crops like German potatoes and Japanese rice without being directly lethal to humans. The first synthetic herbicide—2,4-D—was developed during that period. It didn't kill potatoes, rice, or other grass-like plants, such as corn. However, it controlled other broadleaf plants that grew in those fields. In 1945, that potential weapon was marketed under the product name Weedone for broadleaf weed control in wheat and corn fields.

Arguably, this is the pivotal moment when weeds became enemies to be vanquished rather than wild plants to be used, tolerated, or manually controlled. Over the ten years following the release of Weedone, the word *weed* gradually began cropping up in the titles of agricultural education programs. Eventually, weed management became the focus of agricultural training.

In the years since, synthetic weed control has completely altered the way we farm. Nearly all crops in industrialized countries are grown using herbicides. You can also find an astounding array of herbicide products for use in home gardens. Remarkably, though, even over seventy years later, 2,4-D is the number three most used herbicide behind glyphosate and atrazine, with dicamba running a close fourth.

In response to the nearly universal use of herbicide in farming, over 260 persistent, globally widespread species of weeds have developed resistance to these products. That spiny amaranth I mentioned earlier joined the glyphosate resistance in 2012. It grows rampantly in crop fields near my house and a few years ago made its way to my yard, where I controlled it easily using organic methods.

Ragweed, a pollen-producing plant known to cause allergies in 15 percent of Americans, joined the resistance back in 2004. Thanks to that and climate change, ragweed is now more broadly distributed and has a longer pollen producing season. It's become a real pain for allergy sufferers, according to the US Environmental Protection Agency (EPA). It also found its way to my yard in cover crop seeds bought from a farm supply store. I use it as greens for my compost pile.

Due to ever-increasing herbicide resistance, farmers are being trained to cycle through several different herbicides rather than using just one product multiple times. Similar to crop rotation, changing products confuses pesky weeds and slows their adaptation to new conditions. However, even product rotation is becoming less effective.

Home gardeners are also reporting herbicide resistance. Many conventional gardeners have resorted to using multiple products with greater frequency, spending

A traditional "three sisters" garden.

more on herbicides, or hiring professionals to spray their yards with more varied chemicals to counter the challenges.

The environmental costs of long-term herbicidal wars on weeds are also increasing. Fewer insects, less plant diversity, less arable land, less safe drinking water, more illness, more resistant superweeds, and more climate-altering carbon released into the air are some of the emerging problems. Personally, after learning about these issues, I became herbicide-resistant back in 2008. That's the year I gave up all herbicides in my garden and began eating organic food. Now, many people are beginning to believe that, like the Romans, we might be sowing the seeds of our own destruction with our modern weeding and other agricultural practices.

I could spend the rest of the book detailing the risks and challenges related to herbicides. But that's not the point of this book. The primary reason I shared this history isn't to sow fear for the future or disparage farmers, whom I respect deeply. It's to highlight the fact that our current attitude toward weeds is just an historical blip. It represents a less than 70-year detour in a 200,000-year history of coexisting with a wide variety of wild plants.

There's no doubt that, since the advent of farming, weed removal has been a pain in the back. Unfortunately, that's resulted in slavery, serfdom, and forced or cheap labor being considered necessary for agriculture. But we don't have to do back-breaking manual labor or use herbicides to resist weeds in our home gardens.

We can go forward to a new era of weed management in collaboration with nature. We can leverage the incredible knowledge we've gained through scientific research of plants, soil, and their ecological interactions thanks to modern agricultural methods.

We can also embrace the technological breakthroughs that make it possible to use a variety of attractive and labor-saving solutions in our weed-free gardens.

For example, now that we understand the requirements for seed germination for many weed plants, we know that mulch is the best natural tool for controlling them. Nature forms mulches from leaf litter and the bodies of decaying critters. At home, we can choose many different mulches that will effectively prevent seed germination while making our gardens healthier and more beautiful.

I hope that after reading this book, you'll have a sliding scale for weed tolerance that varies throughout your landscape. Small gardens may be less weed-tolerant than larger gardens. Some parts of your garden might be reserved just for your preferred cultivated plants. Other parts, though, will benefit from the inclusion of volunteer and wild plants, even non-native weeds.

It's okay to pick and choose which weeds you welcome and discourage. The key is not to consider the plants invaders in need of killing, but more like uninvited guests. Some you might be happy to see. Others you'll be eager to strategically show the door. All deserve to be cordially received, asked why they showed up, and adroitly extricated or integrated.

This approach will allow you to spend much less time weeding and lots more time in your garden, enjoying your relationship with your plants—both the intentionally planted ones and the volunteers that arrive spontaneously.

THE ORIGIN OF WEEDS

There were no weeds before agriculture because, in nature, there are only plants that fill specific ecological niches. But did the plants we think of as "weeds" today evolve on purpose so as to take advantage of our growing practices? Are they opportunistic survivors in the Darwinian sense? Is nature intentionally trying to thwart us by introducing plants that take over our cultivated land? Or is something even more astounding at work?

About 23,000 years ago humans made their first known attempts to clear land and cultivate plants. Those early efforts failed. Yet, researchers believe that experiment might have been the point in time when "proto-weeds" began preparing to grow well in human-cultivated soil.

Archaeological records suggest that those proto-farmers mostly managed to grow corn cleavers (*Galium tricornutum*) and darnel (*Lolium temulentum*). Since corn cleavers have limited nutritional value and darnel is toxic, they probably weren't grown on purpose. Their seeds might have been planted by accident with other wild grains. Then, those proto-weeds just grew better than other plants. Or, they may have already been growing in those places before the experimental farmers chose to plant there.

Without a time machine, we can't know for certain. But when humans started farming in earnest 11,000 years later, ancestors of corn cleavers and darnel were among the most persistent weeds of cultivated crop fields. They remained problematic for farmers until the synthetic herbicides of the 1950s finally did them in (to the point of endangering corn cleavers in some areas).

Some people consider that proof that the collective and evolutionary intelligence we refer to as nature had an eleven-millennia head start to make weeds great at growing in human-cultivated soil. If you also consider the more recent evidence of weeds becoming herbicide resistant, that sure makes it seems like the plants are fighting against us.

Personally, though, I don't think that perspective gives nature nearly enough credit. Let me offer you another recent example that might illuminate how some plants can so quickly adapt to any changes in their environment—human-made or otherwise.

In 2009, a new noxious weed called teosinte was reported in Europe. Starting around 9,000 years ago, this native of Mexico was farmed for its grain. About 4,500 years ago, it was domesticated into a new species called maize (the plant that produces corn). Then, teosinte fell out of favor as a cultivated crop.

Corn cleavers

Darnel

without becoming maize, grew at high altitudes, and resisted the same herbicides as modern maize cultivars. No one knows exactly how it happened, but this semi-wild, threatened, ancient grain crossed the ocean and became a noxious weed in only a few years. Evolutionary changes like nitrogen fixation and flood tolerance took ages. But teosinte's ability to threaten cultivated corn happened in one human generation.

Turns out, teosinte didn't need an 11,000-year head start to become a weed, just rapid "introgression." That's the technical term for when related plants share their genetic aptitudes back and forth through cross-pollination. Conservationists were worried about teosinte being endangered by corn. Instead, teosinte emerged as a threat to cultivated corn.

Unlike other no longer cultivated crops that went on to became weeds, teosinte moved into less cultivated parts of Mexico. There it honed some evolutionary skills that allowed it to grow well in less cultivated soil.

Despite those natural advantages, teosinte seemed to have no interest in worldwide domination. However, in response to the North American Free Trade Agreement (NAFTA) in 1994, farmers in Mexico began clearing teosinte-occupied lands to grow corn. These new fields started crowding out the re-wilded teosinte. Instances of teosinte and corn maize cross-pollinating became more common.

Conservationists were concerned that teosinte could be crossed-pollinated out of existence by industrial corn or that the loss of habitat would do it in. So, they distributed teosinte seeds to new locations.

Not many years after this, teosinte began growing as a weed in cornfields in Europe. This new teosinte, though, had a few more fancy adaptations. It learned to cross-pollinate with cultivated maize

The fact is nature has been masterfully using cross-pollination as a method for creating plant diversity for 300 million years. Each seed from some cross-pollinated plants can come equipped with different environmental tolerances and aptitudes. Of course, not all will grow well in every situation. Yet, if a few do, they will live to seed again and again, until they eventually become weeds.

Teosinte was like a sleeper agent, just waiting for some new bit of intel to trigger it into action. How many more sleeper plants are out there waiting for a new opportunity to cross-pollinate, seed, and become the next new weed to worry about?

There are currently 391,000 distinct, known species of plants, and countless variations within each species, with more to be discovered. When you add that to factors like cross-pollination and the mind-blowing numbers of genetically unique seeds wild plants can self-sow, the odds that nature will produce some winners in ANY situation are high. It's like nature is playing the lottery by entering every possible number combination every single time.

PART ONE

WEED
PREVENTION

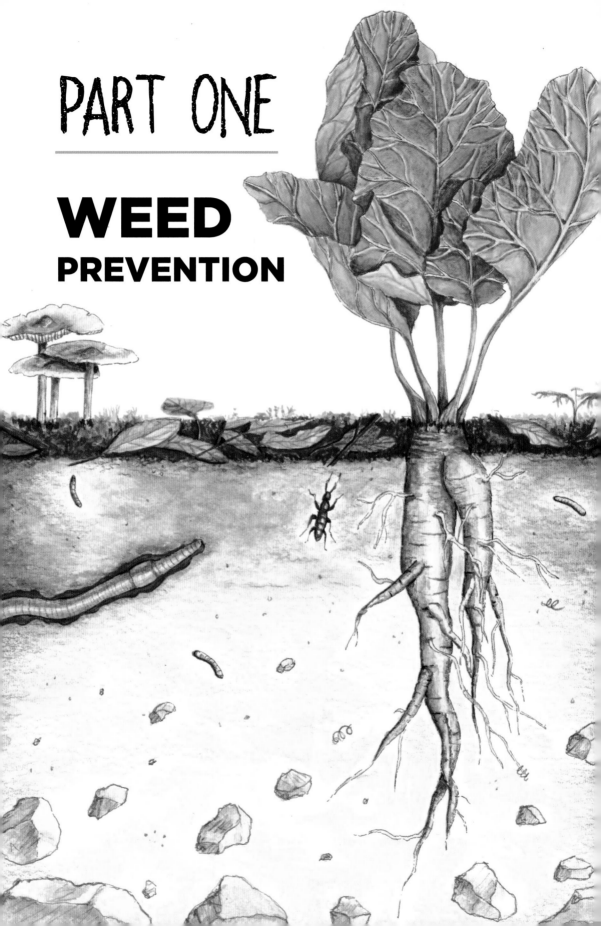

Prevention is the act of stopping something from happening, and it's the single most critical component of weed-free gardening. Weed-free gardening starts with understanding weed behavior and identifying specific risk points for invasions. Then, you can decide on reasonable, strategic actions to prevent those unwanted future outcomes.

That progression of steps seems simple enough in theory. Unfortunately, many of us cut to the solutions part of the process before understanding the real problem. As a result, we take nonstrategic actions that waste time and exacerbate the situation.

Consider, for a moment, a non-garden-related example. If I leave a steak unattended on the coffee table at dog nose height and then let my dogs loose in the room, what will happen? You guessed it! They'd eat the steak. How would you prevent that from happening? Easy. . . don't leave a steak on the coffee table.

Likewise, when deer eat our unprotected plants, they may seem like pests. However, we've just left the deer equivalent of a steak unprotected. The obvious answer to prevent deer from eating our plants is to keep plants out of reach of deer. Protecting a landscape, though, is harder than moving a steak. So, deer get labeled as pests.

The same basic idea applies to weeds. Bare, underoccupied, or heavily fertilized soil is like a steak for weeds—only WAY BETTER. Soil isn't a one-time meal. It's a place to settle down, harvest a continuous supply of free food and water, start a photosynthesis factory, participate in social networks using the rhizosphere (the place where plant roots and soil life collaborate), raise baby plants, and live a happy life. Open soil is like a move-in ready, self-sufficient homestead with free Internet.

> "Prevention is the single most critical component of weed-free gardening."

One of the creators of the permaculture philosophy, Bill Mollison, is credited with giving voice to the idea that in our landscapes, the problem is often the solution. When it comes to weeds, I totally agree. We often garden in ways that create and exacerbate weed invasions by leaving soil bare or unoccupied or by inviting weeds in with other mistakes. Thankfully, our gardening practices can also be the solution when it comes to managing our weeds organically.

Weed prevention starts by acknowledging the ways we encourage weeds in our gardens. Here are some of our most common gardening mistakes that cause weeds.

- We garden where other plants were already established without removing them or actively preventing their return.

- We expose existing seeds stored in the soil with our tilling, harvesting, and weeding practices.

- We leave soil unprotected by not keeping it densely planted or sufficiently mulched.

- We apply too much fertilizer to the surface of soil, which in turn acts like a free buffet for fast-growing, nutrient-hungry weeds.

- We water the top few inches (approximately 7.5 cm) of soil, too often creating ideal conditions for running or self-layering plants to spread.

- We water too shallow and too infrequently for our moisture-loving plants to set deep roots and hold their ground against weeds.

- We don't address drainage problems before we plant and end up with overly dry or wet soil that serves as a breeding ground for weeds that arrive to correct those situations.

- We try to grow plants in unsuitable locations and inappropriate climate conditions or neglect them, then assume it's the weeds' faults when our plants don't grow.

- We don't realize descriptions like "easy to grow" or "fast-growing" are code for "may become a weed unless you control the spread."

- We bring in seeds, soil, potted plants, and other purchases that contain weeds and sow our own problem plants.

- We fail to adjust our gardening practices when changes in our environment necessitate it.

Fundamentally, to be weed-free gardeners, we need to stop blaming plants for taking over and instead look at ways to make soil less attractive to weeds. We also need to think of the garden as a habitat for plants and other critical life forms within a larger ecological system.

A good place to start is by studying the plants you consider weeds in your landscape now. Use those pesky plants to get comfortable asking and answering these three key weed prevention questions.

Three Key Weed Prevention Questions

1) How did these weeds get here?

2) Can I prevent them from spreading or showing up again?

3) How will I fill or protect this niche going forward?

Using these simple questions can help you determine effective and ecologically focused weed prevention methods for your garden. Let's take a closer look at how to strategically answer these questions.

There's no room for weeds in this raised bed filled with grapes, honeyberry, and oregano.

My great Pyrenees puppy, Luna, is natural-born seed spreader, which is one reason she's not allowed in my vegetable garden where I have limited weed tolerance.

How Weeds Get into Our Landscapes

The first question is usually the easiest to answer because there are three main ways that weeds get into our landscape.

1) They are already present in the soil.

2) They are brought in by natural forces, such as pets, wildlife, wind, and water flow or colonization (spreading by rhizomes, solons, runners, layering, and self-sowing).

3) They come in with seed/plant purchases or gifts.

Identifying the most likely source of weed outbreaks can help you narrow down the tactics and will be effective for control. That will also answer the second question about whether you can prevent them from showing up again.

For the first two types—weeds that are already present or brought in by natural forces—maintenance tactics targeted toward suppression and continuous control will be essential to keep them from getting a roothold in your garden. Most of this book is devoted to managing those kinds of weeds, since they are the most prevalent in our landscapes.

With bought-in or brought-in weeds, though, you can manage those risks immediately. Let's look at some common scenarios that lead to new weed problems and ways to address them.

This bare soil will be filled in with a broad array of weeds in no time.

When I bought this plant three days earlier, there were no visible weeds. After watering and waiting a few days, weeds in the pot are germinating.

Problem: *The Transplant Takeover*

You planted a gorgeous new perennial plant in your garden and now the area around it is full of weeds. If those weeds aren't cropping up in other locations, they were either disturbed by digging or in the pot and planted by accident.

With a weed-free gardening approach, you know in advance that soil disturbance triggers weed seed germination. Also, just because potted plants are picked free of weeds to make them attractive, doesn't make them weed-free. Luckily, you don't have to wait for weeds to happen after transplanting. You can mulch preemptively.

MUSHROOM COMPOST

Mushroom compost is my favorite for this purpose. To grow mushrooms for human consummation on substrates like manure or wood chips, mushroom growers pasteurize it to remove pathogens. That also kills weeds. The mushrooms are grown in that substrate, which is kept moist for months in lowlight conditions where weeds germinate and then die from light deprivation. Any plants that do grow are picked out by the growers.

After the mushrooms are harvested, the substrate is decomposed into compost. It gets sold as "mushroom compost" at garden centers. Pasteurization and mushroom production reduce the beneficial biological life and nutrients. So mushroom compost has fewer nutrients than other forms of compost. But that's exactly what makes it wonderful mulch, too. The lower fertility ensures that weeds don't think of it as a smorgasbord.

WEED WHACK!

POST-DISTURBANCE PROTECTION

To keep weed seeds from germinating after disturbances, use 2 inches (5 cm) of mushroom compost, or other weed-free organic mulch, as topdressing over the affected areas after planting. Don't apply directly around plant stems or trunks, as they can rot.

Mushroom compost also makes a perfect topdress for direct-sowing seeds in raised beds. Spread organic slow-release fertilizer over the surface of the bed, and then apply 1 inch (2.5 cm) of mushroom compost. Plant seeds directly in the compost and water often. The seedlings may take a few extra days to get started because of the low nutrients in the mushroom compost. However, once they grow through to the nutrient-rich soil below, they'll take off in the protected soil.

PASTEURIZE SOIL MIXES

You can also pasteurize soil amendments at home. Bake moist, covered compost or soil mixes on a sheet tray at 160°F (71°C) for 60 minutes. Or simmer them in water at the same temperature and time. Then strain. For larger quantities, boil the material in a 50-gallon (189-L) metal drums over outdoor propane burners.

Pasteurizing soil mixes as a planting medium reduces the risk of fungal pathogen problems, like damping off disease that kills seedlings. Remember, though, any pasteurized organic matter needs time to recharge with soil life. When you water, use organic fertilizers, such as fish emulsion, sea kelp, or compost tea, to supply nutrients and increase biological life in the meantime.

CARDBOARD COVER

Using pasteurized compost as a mulch is perfect for suppressing weed seed germination anytime you disturb the soil or start new plants. However, pieces of rhizomes or roots, not removed before planting, can grow right through mulch. Plus rhizomes can spread through mulch and tack down from neighboring plants.

If you suspect your new transplant or planting location contains more persistent weeds, put down a layer of cardboard before the mulch. Use a solid piece with a planting hole cut out. Or overlap the edges between cardboard pieces by a couple of inches. On a slope, the top piece should always face downhill.

A cover of mulch will prevent light dependent Goldenrod seeds from germinating. But existing plants also spread by rhizomes. Remove all visible rhizomes in your bed before planting. Then put down a layer of cardboard under your mulch to prevent residual rhizome pieces from regenerating into new plants.

Keep a close eye on the root zone after planting and quickly remove any weeds that break ground or spread into the area.

Sometimes some plants have so much weedy potential that prevention may need to take more drastic measures. For example, dividing in-ground plants or digging up and moving plants from weedy areas is pretty much guaranteed to be weed-making work. In that case, try root washing.

ROOT WASHING

Root washing is primarily used with perennials like trees, shrubs, woody stemmed herbs, or dormant plants. Some annuals won't survive this process. It can also be beneficial for plants that are rootbound in their containers. Ideally, it should be done in cooler temperatures when plants are dormant or not likely to face heat stress.

Put your plant roots in a tub and gently pour or spray cool water through their roots to remove existing soil. For tightly bound roots, soaking for 10 minutes increases root pliability. Careful agitation using your fingertips can work free clumps with minimal breakage.

After washing, replant immediately in prepared soil. Mulch and monitor as usual. Keep those plants well-watered until they grow in. It can take weeks to months for recovery, depending on the time of year, growth habit of the plant, and soil quality.

Use a gentle tug test to check for root connectivity to the soil. A well-rooted plant will resist being pulled.

Root washing can give weed-infested or rootbound plants a fresh start when replanting in a new location.

BUY BARE ROOT PLANTS

Another option for mass plantings of deciduous perennials, such as starting a new hedge, backyard vineyard, or a mini-orchard, is to buy bare root plants. The plants are uprooted when leafless and dormant, root washed, and shipped without soil.

Bare root plants should be replanted before they break dormancy. Also, roots need to be kept continuously moist from when dug until well-rooted again. Expect bare root plants to require extra care for at least a full year after planting. Buy plants with warranties in case they don't take.

Mulching, root washing, and bare root planting prevent weed outbreaks caused by transplanting. But there are other regular garden inputs and purchases that require conscientious weed-free approaches, too.

Problem:
Soil Amendment Outbreaks

Organic gardening requires high-quality soil to do the work of nourishing plants. If you don't have that to start, you'll need to bring in lots of organic matter in the form of compost, soil mixes, mulches, manures, and more for the first few years of gardening in a new location. However, every application of organic matter also comes with the potential for new weed outbreaks.

I still remember the year I accidentally planted hairy bittercress (*Cardamine hirsute*). Those lovely little plants didn't sow directly in the mulch they came in because undecomposed wood shreds aren't their ideal planting medium. But their seeds dropped along my dirt paths as I forked the mulch onto my beds.

When they first appeared in late fall, the plants were so tiny and stayed that way so long, I didn't realize I had a weed problem. After a few warm days in late February, thousands of them stood 3 inches tall (7.5 cm) and wide, covering the ground like a well-regimented army.

If I'd controlled them then, by mowing or hoeing, that would have been the end of the problem. Yet, they were so stunning in winter and so delicious, I let them go to seed. Then I discovered their mature seed pods are spring-loaded. They catapult seeds as far as 15 feet (4.5 m) when dry. Now, they come up all over the place in fall and grow through until spring.

I share this self-incriminating example because the truth is weed seeds in soil amendments are never the real issue. The problem starts when gardeners don't control new weeds before they sow seeds or spread by other methods. If you catch weeds early before the roots are deep, a gentle pass with a hoe will make quick work of them with minimal soil disturbance.

The delicate white flower and wispy seed pods of bittercress are so prolific they seem like leaves. They also pack a projectile punch that can propel new potential weeds up to 15 feet (4.6 m).

I call this stirrup hoe my weed decapitator and this is what it does to hairy bittercress (*Cardamine hirsute*).

This is my favorite tool for general weeding. It comes in standing form too, but I prefer hand-to-weed combat with plants I've declared weeds.

HULA OR STIRRUP HOE

This type of hoe is wonderful for removing shallow-rooted weeds, such as for regular use between rows in a vegetable garden. It's also good for deeper annuals with rosette-type leaves. It chops their leafy tops off right below the crown while leaving their roots underground for minimal soil disturbance.

BLADED HOES

There are also a range of bladed hoes that slice through weeds above or just below the surface of the soil. Some have a loop like a hula hoe, combined with a blade. Others are solid. Some have pie-shaped heads with the point facing forward for pushing through weed crowns. Others have the same shape with the wide side of the pie slice blade facing forward for slicing through a wider swath of weeds. These are all used for surface hoeing of annual weeds.

RAKE HOE COMBO

My favorite bladed hoe is handheld and comes with a rake. The rake is good for gently wiggling out dense root systems without excessive soil disturbance. Just use your fingers to hold soil in place as you wiggle the rake tips under the crown. The hoe blade hacks through the thick crowns of thistles.

DIGGING HOES

Digging hoes are typically used in dry, compacted soils to clear between rows. Their heavy metal heads and right angle make them almost hammer like. I've never used one. But I hear they're common in dry regions.

Hoes can make quick work of snuffing out seedlings and dealing with mature, shallow-rooted plants. But if you don't want to be hoeing all year long, there are some other methods you can use to reduce weed germination in fresh-applied soil amendments using nature's intelligence.

BIOMIMICRY— BE LIKE NATURE!

"Biomimicry" is a term used to describe copying nature's methods to achieve human goals. For example, nature amends soil with organic matter, such as leaves, dead things, and manure from wildlife. It just does it very slowly in such tiny increments that the soil life quickly uses it. It's kind of like compost on demand, and it means there's no buffet of nutrients ready and waiting at the soil's surface for weeds to consume.

Also, nature applies organic matter under the shade protection of already existing plants and leaf cover. That natural shade reduces light transmission, which naturally reduces germination. The leaf matter provides a roof over the soil to encourage soil life to surface even in less-than-ideal warm or cool conditions.

When we apply soil amendments at home, it's often done in bigger quantities because we want faster results. Still, we can emulate these ideas for better results.

WEED WHACK!

COVER CROPPING

For compost or topsoil amendments, cover cropping after application can help integrate those amendments into the existing soil quickly. This involves applying the amendment and immediately overseeding with a short season annual that grows quickly to shade soil. Plus, the root mass underground offers shelter to microlife as they integrate the new organic matter into existing soil. Those roots also keep nutrients from washing away until that rich matter can be stored deeper in the soil.

When your plants show signs of flowering, mow them down to prevent seeding. Then let the mowed leaves and stems stay as a natural leaf mulch to preserve moisture.

After a round of cover crops, you can safely plant your long-term plants with much less risk for weed problems. Alternatively, if weed pressure is still intense, repeat with another round or two of different cover crops until the weeds time out (see page 106-107).

Cover crop plants are nutrient launderers selected specifically for their ability to root quickly and use up nutrients that would otherwise become airborne or wash away. Then, as they decompose, those nutrients go back into the soil.

That buys time for soil integration and keeps it from becoming weed feed. Under newly planted perennials, though, that makes them competitors for the same resources. If you want to plant perennials immediately after amending soil, try the method featured on the following page instead.

WEED WHACK!

LIVING MULCH

Many of the seasonally appropriate flowering annuals you find at the garden center are specifically designed to occupy space under and around perennials without competing for root space or nutrients. They act as a living mulch around your plant, occupying the soil at the surface and reducing weed germination.

Seasonal annuals are shallow-rooted and require regular care. Their presence reminds you to go out to your beds so you can water and weed.

Those annuals stay shallow-rooted, which means they require regular watering to stay lovely. Wilted plants can serve as a reminder to deep water around your perennials. Also, weeds stand out against a backdrop of decorative annuals, encouraging you to weed that area regularly.

As those annuals die, leave them in place as organic matter so the nutrients they borrowed can be returned to feed those perennials down the road. If you don't want those annuals to self-sow in the future, choose sterile hybrids.

There are also lots of perennial ground covers that can be planted under taller perennials for long-term weed prevention. Perennial ground covers grow deeper than seasonal annuals. Wait to plant until after your other perennials are settled in.

TARP TOP OR CARDBOARD COVER

If planting isn't immediately possible, such as in cold weather, deeply water the area where the soil amendment was applied. Then cover it loosely with a tarp so air can still get in. The moisture and darkness will encourage soil life into the upper inches of soil. But the tarp will block light so weeds can't germinate.

In hot, sunny weather, tarping will discourage soil life from coming to the surface because it makes it more likely for them to roast or suffocate. Instead, use cardboard held in place with a few rocks to create a cool zone for soil workers to start integrating organic matter under cover.

These examples reduce weed seed germination. However, they serve an even more important role of encouraging soil life to come to the surface and incorporate those amendments into the rhizosphere.

Perennial ground covers like these are as easy to grow as weeds. They act as a natural mulch year-round but are prettiest in late winter and early spring.

To Dig or Not to Dig

Once upon a time, digging to incorporate soil amendments was a standard practice. Organic gardeners were encouraged to apply amendments and then till the soil to mix them in. The theory was that by mixing them into the soil, the nutrients would be in the root zone and stay put until needed.

Today, we know that's not how soil works. Particle size, moisture content, biological life, soil composition, and other factors impact whether those amendments become integrated. In the wrong situation, digging amendments in can create anaerobic bogs or they may just float back up.

Additionally, soil research indicates those kind of cataclysmic digging events disrupt soil life networks. They bring seeds back to the surface to germinate. Plus, exposing subsoil to air reduces moisture content and causes nutrients and carbon to become airborne or wash away.

Today, organic gardeners are moving toward no-dig methods. Unfortunately, no-dig isn't immediately compatible with soil that is seriously compacted or structured in impermeable layers. Those areas can become bog-prone or an erosion hazard when amendments are layered on top.

A simple stake test can help you decide if your soil is no-dig ready. Hammer a metal stake into the ground during dry conditions. If it goes in down to at least 8 inches (20 cm) with relative ease, throughout your bed areas, your soil is probably permeable enough for no-dig gardening. If your soil doesn't pass the stake test, you may need to do a little digging to find out why.

Also, adding amendments on slopes just leads to runoff rather than integration. Even if your soil is permeable, it also needs to be level enough for amendments to stay put for months until they're integrated. If your garden is sloped, you'll need to level, terrace, or create other water infiltration systems to ensure amendments don't erode.

On minor slopes, use untreated burlap to hold amendments in place. That will erode in a couple of months. But by then, your plants and soil will have started to stabilize the organic matter.

The ultimate goal of weed-free gardening is to minimize soil disturbance. Therefore, doing as little routine digging as possible is key to weed-free gardening success. But an absolute no-dig policy in a new garden is only practical on mostly flat areas with permeable soil.

Problem: *Toxic Invaders*

Herbicides are now ubiquitous in industrial agriculture. They're even used in managed forests. Unfortunately, that means industrially produced soil amendments and mulches come with residues from those toxic chemicals. For example, baled straw and hay are typically grown in fields treated with herbicides. Those plants can uptake herbicides into their stems. Then, cutting, drying, and baling preserves herbicide residues in those materials until they reach your landscape.

When you apply them on your garden beds, residues leach into your soil by rain and decomposition. In high doses, they can stress or kill your existing plants and decrease microlife in the soil. When plants can't grow due to herbicide residues, then weed invasion risks increase. Also, those amendments may come with their own collection of herbicide-resistant weed seeds.

The fact is, most amendments, even some certified organic, have minor toxic residues. They're just literally in everything at this point, including waterways and irrigation water sources. Luckily, the extensive microlife communities that decompose plant matter and incorporate soil amendments also help mitigate risks from toxins. There are also ways to manage your risks before you apply.

WEED WHACK!

BE INFORMED

Though they may cause short-term disturbances, many herbicides time out quickly in healthy, organic soil. Thriving biological communities can make quick work of cleanup. Unfortunately, several years ago I applied cow manure compost that contained toxic residues with long-term consequences. That's when I learned that herbicides in the aminopyralid family that include products like Milestone, GrazonNext HL, or Chaparral, as well as picloram products like Tordon, are specifically labeled by the manufacturer as unsuitable for use—directly or indirectly—in broadleaf garden areas, like vegetable gardens. This warning includes hay, straw, and manure from livestock that ate them. It also applies to compost made with any of those things.

Unfortunately, compost makers and hay and straw bale sellers don't always know that their products contain these garden hazards. The only surefire advice I can give you to prevent weed outbreaks from potentially toxic herbicide residues is to try before you apply. The technical term for this process is "bioassay."

WEED WHACK!

BIOASSAY BEFORE YOU APPLY

For things that you can't plant directly in (wood mulch, stone dust, crop residues, or leaf mold) start some sacrificial seedlings in a pot of your garden soil. Fast germinators like mustard, radish, peas, zinnia, or other broadleaf, non-grasses will work for this.

Simultaneously, fill a container about one-tenth of the way up with your soil amendment and fill the rest to the top with water. Use the strained water from the container to water your seedlings until they've put out a few sets of leaves. (Note: Don't put a lid on the container or the water will stagnate.)

For soil amendments or planting medium (raised bed mix, topsoil, or compost) start seedlings directly in small pots of those materials. Be careful not to overwater since those mixes are better at retaining moisture than seed starting mix.

For my annual bulk materials deliveries, I use a half gallon (1.9 L) mason jar and some pea seeds to make sure there are no contaminants before I apply any to my planting areas.

If you see any signs of malformed leaves, stunting, or death, do more research and testing before using those amendments.

These tests are nonscientific and therefore not perfect preventative measures. For me, though, they've steered me clear of several safety hazards in soil amendments.

THE WEED SEEDS WE SOW

Another way we sow our own weed problems is with our seed purchases. Sometimes just looking at the seeds in your packet and picking out any that are noticeably different before sowing can help. However, there's a phenomenon called Vavilovian mimicry (for the geneticist who identified this pattern) that can make weed seeds indistinguishable from cultivated seeds.

The process happens at first by chance. A few weeds make it to maturity by blending in with the existing crops. Their seeds get harvested with the crop. Most of the weed seeds get sorted out at winnowing since they look different than the target harvest. However, a few weed seeds come out misshapen or a different color and make it through the sorting process.

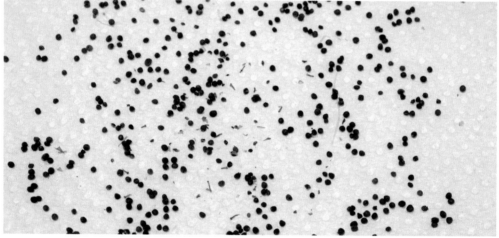

Top: Visual seed inspection works for large, distinctly shaped seeds like these cucumber seeds. But not for all seeds.

Bottom: These seeds came from one mustard plant I harvested by hand. Their natural disposition towards varied seed color and shape could allow weed seeds to hide in this mix.

Those weed seeds get planted with that same crop again the next time. A few more similarly sized plants hide in plain sight by appearing similar in some way to the crops grown. Their seeds get harvested, too. This time, more of their seeds resemble the crop seed. In a few generations, the weed has adapted to blend in with the crop and make seeds that are nearly indistinguishable by standard sorting mechanisms. These weeds then get sent out to seed buyers everywhere.

Besides Vavilovian mimicry risks, some weed seeds are too small to be winnowed out. Truthfully, the risk of accidentally sowing weed seeds is ever-present and hard to avoid. But there are ways to manage risks.

For things like wildflower mixes and cover crops, used over a large area, the seed packager will indicate the percentage of weed seeds that are in your package. Unfortunately, they don't tell you what kind of weeds they are.

In that case, you may want to pre-germinate a portion of the package. Identify the seedlings and weedlings as they come up. Then you'll be ready to spot and pick out the weedlings when they grow in your plot and not accidentally pull up the wildflower seedlings in the process.

WEED WHACK!

DON'T DIRECT SOW

In small gardens, starting seeds in cells or pots makes weed control at the time of planting easy. Simply pick out any weedlings that emerge with the seedlings.

PRE-PLANTING GERMINATION

To do a pre-germination planting test, scatter sow part of your packet of seeds into shallow trays with pre-moistened potting soil. Dust the seeds with soil to cover and mist with water. Keep this in a warm, well-lit location. Mist regularly for a week or two to find out what comes up. Weeds usually sprout first with this method.

You can also use this pre-germination method to find out which weeds are lurking in your compost. Just skip the planting part and moisten a tray of compost to see what grows in it.

Weed Realities

Beyond the weed problems we create with purchases, amendments, and digging, weed seeds can also get carried in by birds, flow in with storm runoff, catch a ride on animal fur, or blow in on a gust of wind. Other plants may run underground. Some plants reproduce from root cuttings that stay dormant until soil disturbance triggers them into action. Weeds can even "walk" to a new location by leaning over and self-layering.

You can stop some weeds from getting in and spreading with the kind of preventative actions we've just covered. But unfortunately, most weeds aren't so easily preventable; nature is extremely adept at supplying plants to solve soil problems and in response to environmental events out of our control.

The ability to prevent them from spreading or showing up depends on how effective you are at filling niches as a general gardening habit before nature does. Also, the routine gardening practices you use and how you manage your soil matters immensely.

Weed Control

Ultimately, effective weed control requires good soil preparation, soil protection, and continuous weed life cycle disruption. In general, the more time spent on soil preparation and protection, the less time you'll need to spend on disruption. Also, the disruption work tends to decline over time if you keep at it.

SOIL PREPARATION

If you move into a furnished house, you won't try to put your sofa in the exact same spot as where an existing sofa already sits. You'd do something about the old sofa first, like clean it, give it away, or move it. You'd probably also do some housekeeping to make the place move-in ready.

The same idea applies to a new garden. You can't just put new plants where old plants are already growing and hope for the best. You must address the plant life present in your landscape and do a little housekeeping to get started.

The challenge is that existing plants aren't as easy to see or remove as a sofa. Also, some weeds are like Medusa—you cut off one stem and sixteen grow back. The hard truth that many gardeners don't like to hear is that the most persistent weeds will require specific knowledge and some clever gardening skills to eradicate entirely. It can also take several years to manage those more persistent weeds.

WEED WHACK!

POT-HOLE COMPOSTING

If weed removal leaves a large hole, backfill it with compostable materials, such as kitchen scraps, livestock manure, shredded paper, cardboard, and other compostable materials. Then top it with a couple of inches (approximately 5 cm) of soil. If you have pets, put a planter pot or paver stone over the area to discourage digging. In a few months these materials will be decomposed into the soil and will feed nearby plants.

Pot-hole composting is an easy method to compost directly in the ground without the risk or work of digging a long trench.

You can't just put down a little paper and some compost and plant over in every situation. You may have to do some digging first. Sometimes, that digging is deep research to identify and understand a weed and make a plan to minimize its presence in your garden. Other times, you may have to do some actual digging.

Digging always increases the risk that other weeds will invade the area. However, if research reveals that the only way to control a specific weed is to dig it up and eradicate it entirely, pick the least invasive tool possible for removal.

 TOOL BAR

THE HORI HORI KNIFE

This digging knife has a shovel-like shape, pointy digging tip, and a serrated side to use as a cutting tool. It works great for removing shallow taproots with minimal disturbance to the surrounding soil. Find the crown of the plant, move the leaves out of the way, then cut a circle around the root area.

Like coring an apple, once you've made a complete cut, pull the entire weed out. If it doesn't come easily, you probably have a deeper root. Use the tip of the knife to cut through the root. Once the shallower part of the plant is out of the way, you may be able to make a deeper cut with your digging knife to finish the job. If not, then escalate to the next two tools.

Note: For less aggressive root regenerators, such as an already flowered short-lived perennial or annual weed, partial root removal might be enough to prevent regrowth.

THE DRAIN SPADE

A drain spade is a long, narrow shovel with a rounded shape that resembles the hori hori knife, only longer. Use it the same way as the digging knife to core around the root, then pull out the entire plant.

ROUND POINT SHOVEL

For taprooted plants with roots that fork or plants with thick fibrous roots, you may need to use a round point shovel. Dig patches around the crown of the plant and remove root parts as you free them up. After clearing the main roots, use the digging knife or drain spade to get out thin off-shoots.

Digging large or deep holes always involves major soil disturbance. Be ready with a replacement plant to fill the niche. Or use that space for pot-hole composting.

Lambsquarters (*Chenopodium album*) are a tasty, nutritious, and beautiful food source. Some call them a weed; I call them an easy-to-grow edible that I remove, like other greens or herbs, when the plant starts to bolt.

Removal by digging works when you can see the plant. Unfortunately, unless you have dead soil, there are also future plants underground that you can't see yet. Seasonal plants that die back in winter, root pieces or rhizomes, and dormant seeds stored in your soil seed bank may just be waiting for ideal conditions to grow.

Plants that start from buried root cuttings or rhizomes that regenerate underground can take months to years to resurface. Plus, some seeds can remain dormant for years. For example, lambsquarters (*Chenopodium album*), a notorious and delicious vegetable garden weed, can produce 75,000 seeds per plant. Each of those seeds can have unique germination triggers, such as temperature fluctuations, soil nitrate levels, sudden exposure to light, and more. Weed seeds with these kind of widely varied dormancy periods can take decades to time out.

Fortunately, many weed seeds don't go dormant. They stay alert watching for signals to trigger germination. If those conditions don't occur, the seeds use up their stored energy waiting and lose viability. These seeds are also called auto-germinating. They tend to be the most prolific in gardens. But they are also the easiest to control by covering them with mulch to prevent germination until they time out.

Stinging nettle (*Urtica dioica*), a useful but potentially painful-to-pull mint family weed, falls into the auto-germinating category. The seeds just need light and consistent moisture to germinate. Mulching over it will suppress it from starting by seed. However, it also spreads by rhizomes. So, it's a plant that you may want to use multiple control methods with, such as building a deep and wide raised bed over the area, then also carefully removing any of the rhizomes that run out the sides until they time out.

Stinging nettle (*Urtica dioica*) is a useful herb if you make herbal medicines. It's also wonderful for use in making compost teas. Just use care when handling because it's called stinging for a reason.

SOIL CARE

Soil is not just a planting medium. It's a living system full of various life forms. As such, soil care is one of the most exciting and complex parts of weed-free gardening. We're going to get into lots of specifics on that in Part 2: Maintenance. For now, just know that with good preparation and long-term soil care, your plants will grow even better, your garden will be more beautiful and productive, and you'll spend less time on weed prevention.

LIFE CYCLE DISRUPTION

Being a disruptor is quite trendy these days—all the venture capitalist–funded tech people want to be known for disrupting the status quo. But good gardeners are the ultimate disruptors. We do extensive overhauling of the existing environment as part of soil preparation. Then we put it back together in new and exciting ways using plants and other methods of soil protection. After that, we continuously disrupt weedlings before they get a roothold in our gardens. Well, that's what we should be doing. This is where gardeners often lose steam. To be a true disruptor, you must stay on top of the competition long-term.

We already know weeds aren't the enemy. But they do have a way of poking holes in our best-laid weed-prevention plans when we let our guard/garden down. For example, fair weather gardeners who don't get outdoors in hot weather may not notice nature's emergency weather responder-type weeds popping up. I totally get it! I also like to sit in the shade sipping iced tea rather than scorch in the garden pulling weeds. But frankly, so do most of your plants. Pretty much only weeds can thrive in extended heat.

The fact is, your garden should never be so unbearable that you can't visit—or weeds will. That's why a huge part of weed-free gardening involves improving soil to hold more water, support more plants, and keep the entire garden cooler as a result. It takes a few years for this transformation to happen though. So, in the meantime, disrupt weeds in the morning or evening until your soil gets its chill on. Then, you'll be able to do a lot more iced tea sipping in your weed-free garden down the road.

Soil preparation, soil care, and weed disruption are the basic tools we use to avoid having to spray toxic herbicides in our garden. More importantly, though, like seeing the forest for the trees, weed-free gardening is also very much about seeing the garden for the weeds.

Unfortunately, all the things we thought we knew about our climate and weather are becoming less relevant. Weeds, though, as the most immediately responsive plants in our landscape, are an incredible resource to help us understand changes in real time while we garden.

Figuring out why certain weeds come rather than others or noting patterns in their size, number, diversity, and root structure can help us better manage our gardens.

This little diverse, healthy weedscape tells me the soil is ready to be used for more cultivated plants.

Niche Knowledge

Previously I mentioned niches and niche filling. I'm sure you already have a good sense of what that means. But this concept is so central to weed-free gardening that I'd like you to start using it right away to address your weed problems. Here's how.

Identify the weeds that are most persistent, prolific, or problematic in your landscape. Regional weed lists, other gardeners, agricultural offices, phone apps, and broad Internet searches can help you with weed identification. Comparisons of your weed to online photos, illustrations, and detailed plant descriptions can help narrow down a positive ID.

This goosegrass (*Eleusine indica*) is an eyesore in my mulched paths. Light blocking prevents its spread without creating massive soil disturbance, or back injuries, by trying to uproot it.

Next, use the Latin name, not common name, of your weeds to learn as much as you can about them from weed guides or Internet research. Latin names are critical because many weeds share the same common name. For example, goosegrass is a problem for gardeners in my area. But various species of *Acrachne*, *Carex*, *Eleusine*, *Galium*, and *Puccinellia* all use the common name goosegrass.

The goosegrass we worry about, *Eleusine indica*, sets deep and wide roots in clay soil. It's difficult to remove without extensive soil disruption. It attracts flea beetles that quickly move over to cultivated plants. It thrives in dry, fertile, compacted areas of bare soil (like my pathways when they are overdue for more mulch). Pulling them is practically impossible. But a weighted rock, cardboard, or concrete stepping-stones keeps them from seeding. Frost kills them. Then I can mulch to prevent them the next year.

After you have a good understanding of the weed, you can study the area it's growing in and make educated guesses about the conditions that encourage this particular weed. Finally, using that understanding, you can figure out how best to control it and prevent it from returning, while making improvements to support the health of your preferred plants.

Let's look at a few examples to see how this works.

DISTURBED SOILS

Many weeds that show up in our gardens come with descriptions, like thrives in "disturbed soil" such as along roadsides, in crop fields, and on construction sites. Disturbance-triggered weeds are most common after garden renovations or in annual gardens where digging is common.

If your garden has just undergone any kind of disturbance of that sort, then you just need to gently hand-pull these weeds while they're young. Then apply a fresh layer of mulch or compost to prevent more of these weeds from germinating.

If they keep recurring in areas you don't regularly dig or haven't recently disturbed, they could indicate a soil erosion problem. Terracing or growing erosion-preventing plants might be necessary to stop the soil disturbance.

Possibly some critter is repeatedly disturbing the soil too, such as by digging warrens or feeding on grubs. More underground pest prevention might be the answer.

When none of those conditions are present, it can also be an indication of poor soil care, such as too little organic matter, not enough regular watering, no mulch protection, or too few plants to protect the soil. In that case, better soil preparation and strategic planting will fill that niche.

SPECIFIC SOIL QUALITIES

Your research may also give you details on some specific soil quality those weeds prefer. That can help you decide which soil amendments to use. Alternatively, you may decide to select plants that are more likely to thrive in the existing soil.

Rats are a common feature of urban and rural gardens. Their warren digging activities can stir up weed invasions regularly if left uncontrolled.

LOW PH

Not all plants can uptake nutrients when the pH is low and runs acidic. If most of your weeds are known to favor acidic soil, then you've got a low pH problem. You can solve your pH using targeted applications of slow-release lime. Beware, though, any sudden pH changes, such as those from fast-acting lime, are likely to trigger massive weed outbreaks.

Alternatively, you can add compost or biochar to raise the pH while increasing humic content. Even before your soil pH adjusts, adding compost will act as a pH buffer so plants will still grow well even at a less than ideal pH. Be careful when adding lime and compost together, though, as that can add up to more of a pH change than you bargained for.

You can also grow things that like acidic soil. These include mosses, azaleas, rhododendrons, blueberries, cranberries, lingonberries, hollies, heathers, or a handful of other evergreens.

EXCESS MOISTURE

In areas prone to excess moisture, you may find weeds labeled "semi-aquatic" or that are noted for having flood tolerance. A high density of shallow-rooted, large-leaved weeds looking quite perky is also a possible indicator of extra moisture.

If your soil isn't normally boggy, then finding those weeds can indicate a drainage issue. If you've been adding a lot of organic matter, it may mean it's time to grow some deep-rooted plants to incorporate that further into the soil. Or perhaps you need to rake off some of that matter and slow things down until the soil dries out a bit.

It could also indicate changes higher up on your landscape that are increasing the water flow to your garden. That may require addressing drainage before it hits your planting area.

DRY SOIL

In dry soils, scrubby plants with damaged or unattractive leaves are common since dry-loving plants spend less water on leaf maintenance. A lack of plant diversity, low-growing, creeping, sprawling, or prostrate plants are also indicators of nature trying to help preserve limited soil moisture.

Regular watering, using moisture-retentive aged compost, and covering with mulch are niche-filling answers in some cases. But if dryness is due to compaction, then you need to address that before filling the niche. Growing dry-loving plants with penetrative root systems can help solve compaction and drive organic matter and water deeper into the soil profile.

BARE, FERTILE-APPEARING SOIL

When soil is dark and rich and appears fertile but even the weeds are spindly and shallow-rooted, chances are your soil is too alkaline. Confirm this with a pH test. If your pH isn't too high, then it could be an excess of certain nutrients or herbicide toxicity. In that situation, you may need to have a laboratory soil test to track down the issue.

FERTILE SOIL

Weeds that look lush and are slow to flower indicate fertile, moist soil that you ought to be gardening in. If they are growing lushly right in the same soil with your cultivated plants, it means you haven't weeded enough at the weedling stage or forgot to apply mulch. Or perhaps it means you chose to let them grow, like I do with several of the tastiest weeds.

WEED LONGEVITY

As you study your weeds, note whether they are newly arrived or long-established. Weeds can randomly crop up in response to a short-term problem. For example, a lightning strike converts airborne nitrogen into plant-usable nitrogen in an instant. Then, in response, weeds and fungi often erupt over the next few days and weeks. Or extended weather events like droughts or rains can trigger weeds caused by dryness or excess moisture.

If the weed populations seem well-established, there's a good chance the niche they are filling is a permanent one. In that case, use nature's wisdom but pick prettier plants.

Analogous plants aren't your only option for niche-filling. Gardens also need places for gardeners to relax, potting sheds, or other kinds of infrastructure to make them beautiful, useful, and enjoyable. So, your weediest areas might be better suited for something other than garden beds.

WEED WHACK!

TARGETED PLANT SELECTION

Choosing plants that have similar soil and environmental preferences to your happy weeds is an easy way to fill in niches more aesthetically. For example, if your white clover is over a foot tall with lush leaves and abundant flowers or your land is crawling with vining vetches (*Vicia* spp.), then decorative cultivars of false indigo (*Baptisia* spp.) or lupine (*Lupinus* spp.) could be perfect. Those plants also fix nitrogen and protect soil, like clover and vetch. But they're easier to manage and develop deeper roots that can be even more beneficial for long-term soil stability.

Countless cultivated plants are adapted to a wide range of soil types and environmental conditions and can fill niches even better than plants nature chose. That's because nature is limited to what's in the seed bank or circulating nearby. Meanwhile, we can order plants from all over the country. You just need to know the niche, fill them with ideal analogs, and nurture them until they settle in.

This clover is happy and healthy, but ordinary in appearance. Prettier legumes can do the same job with more pizzazz.

SUBSTITUTE THE SERVICE

Perhaps nature repeatedly plants impossible-to-remove sprawling weeds into a hot, dry, compacted, room-sized part of your landscape. You could do massive soil renovation, including tilling, adding organic matter, and cycling through various plants until the soil stabilizes, and then growing some low-water-need, heat-loving plants.

Or you could bring in a load of light-colored river rock and start some rock beds. Rocks protect soil and provide a great mulch for low water-, low nutrient-needing plants.

Horsenettle is an eyesore and problem spreader in poor conditions. In places with diverse plant life and stable soil, it rarely seems to spread and can even be pretty.

This sad little horsenettle started from old seeds buried in my yard. But in this state, it's weak and easy to control by hand pulling.

WEED SERVICES

Nature always seems to keep the soil stocked with all sorts of "fixers," or plants that show up to fix whatever temporary problem has occurred in the soil.

SURVIVALIST WEEDS

When we moved to our homestead, an area of our yard was mostly bare except for sad-looking splotches of horsenettle (*Solanum carolinense*). A falling down grape arbor and sickly vine, plus a raggedy mess of black plastic trash bags, told a tale of failed herbicide and light deprivation warfare. It was obvious this weed was the only survivor of near-total decimation.

Horsenettle survives any situation by developing an extensive, deep taproot system that can grow 3 feet (1 m) deep and over 10 feet (3 m) wide in any direction. New shoots can crop up at any point along the roots if the parent plant is disturbed or endangered. It regenerates from root pieces under 1 inch (2.5 cm) long. Plus, it self-layers like tomato vines in moist soil. If mowed before flowering, growth hormones in its stems cause it to branch and become bushier like pinched herbs.

Its seeds can germinate from 4 inches (10 cm) underground and do so prolifically when soil temperatures fluctuate between 68 and 86°F (20 and 30°C), especially if excess phosphorus is present. That means seeds easily sprout up under mulch in phosphorous-rich garden soil, right in the middle of prime growing season.

If ingested, horsenettle is lethal to livestock and toxic to birds and humans. Plus, as a member of the nightshade family, it hosts insects and diseases that plague tomatoes and potatoes, including wilts, blights, and leaf-eating beetles. Did I mention its stems are barbed more heavily at the base of the plant to prevent hand pulling? In my yard, it made me think of a cross-and-bones danger sign. In fact, scaring off deer and rabbits from grazing that danger zone was likely it's primary niche.

On paper, this seems like a weed you can't control organically. In actuality, it's a weed you can't control with nonorganic methods. Herbicides, tilling, and mowing make it spread. Pre-emergent treatments don't exist. Use of synthetic fertilizers with phosphorous just fuels seed germination and plant growth.

I was daunted by this plant. Still, I had to try. I built a hot compost pile (with internal heat of 135°F [57°C] or above) on top of it to see if heat and compost leachate would kill it. It worked under the pile. Unfortunately, more shoots came up all around the pile. So, I built new piles on top of the new shoots. I also covered the surrounding areas with cardboard to slow down new shoots.

Once the compost cooled and mellowed, I filled the area with a variety of fast-growing herbs like peppermint, oregano, yarrow, and comfrey to speed the soil recovery. It took five years of patient gardening to control the horsenettle. A few new plants still periodically start from old seeds buried in the soil, but they're weakly rooted and easy to pull.

PHYTOREMEDIATORS

Phytoremediation plants also tell tales of toxic soil. They usually show up in large groups and grow while other plants struggle. Many of these plants bioaccumulate those toxic minerals from the soil into their leaves and stems. For example, the Chinese brake fern (*Pteris vittata*) can draw up large amounts of arsenic into its leaves. Certain varieties of mustard (*Brassica juncea*) are good at removing cadmium, lead, and selenium.

Several species of *Ranunculus*, commonly known as buttercups, have been found growing well in toxic sites with excessive heavy metals, such as near paper mills. Early trials have shown them to be potentially useful for phytoremediation after oil spills.

If you suspect plants are doing phytoremediation in your soil, you may need professional assistance to figure out how to solve the issue.

PREPPER PLANTS

Plants with a tendency to hoard nutrients are particularly pesky for conventional gardeners because they often respond to sudden changes in the nutrient profile. For example, quackgrass (*Elymus repens*), a common and difficult-to-control garden weed, makes more rhizomes whenever the soil nutrients start to decline.

In nature, nutrients are normally stable in the soil and only decline when the weather cools and soil life become less active. In annual gardens, though, it can happen any time heavy-feeding plants have growth spurts or flower. Quackgrass then inconveniently hoards exactly when your plants also need those residual nutrients.

Alternatively, when nutrients suddenly increase, such as when fertilizer is added, quackgrass gobbles them up and grows rapidly, again using up nutrients you meant for your plants and making your quackgrass problem bigger.

Organic gardens rely on soil life to make nutrients available to plants on demand, rather than the application of fertilizers. So, nutrient hoarders aren't as problematic in our gardens. But beware when you try to mix and match organic gardening practices with conventional fertilizing. Synthetic fertilizers bypass soil life and can send weeds into a nutrient feeding frenzy. Even fast-acting organic fertilizers, such as blood meal or dried manures, can speed up nutrient cycling in ways that favor those prepper weeds.

Note About Organic Fertilizer

Organic fertilizers are made from organic matter known to contain certain kinds of nutrients. For example, bone meal is ground bones that contain phosphorous and calcium. Blood meal is nitrogen rich blood that's been dried and powdered. Fish emulsion is fish that have been emulsified and fermented in water to extract the naturally occurring nitrogen, phosphorous, and potassium.

Just like synthetic fertilizers, these can trigger weeds in your garden. However, we typically use them in much smaller quantities and in conjunction with other forms of organic matter to mitigate weed risks. We also use them in soil that has more carbon and microlife to store the nutrients quickly. Still, use them sparingly and only when really needed to avoid feeding weeds.

NITROGEN MAKERS

Some plants can fix their own nitrogen by forming relationships with specialized bacteria called rhizobia. The rhizobia colonize the root system of the plant using a series of nodules. They collect non-plant usable nitrogen (N2) from the air in soil. The plant supplies the rest of the materials the rhizobia need to convert that N2 into NH3, a plant-usable form of nitrogen.

Legumes are the most common nitrogen fixers, but some non-legumes have the ability, too. When nitrogen-fixing plants die, or part of their root systems die, the nitrogen nodules decay into the soil and the nitrogen becomes available to other plants.

In that sense, they are often considered beneficial. Yet, most weedy nitrogen fixers just fix enough nitrogen for their own survival in poor-quality soil. They also use other minerals in the soil and take up water. If they are the only plants growing in an area, that likely means you don't have enough carbon content in your soil to bond with nitrogen and store it long-term. As a result, only plants that can make nitrogen will thrive until you improve the soil.

WEED WHACK!

FIX NITROGEN FOR REAL

Though weeds can fix some nitrogen, those small amounts are mostly self-serving. To fix nitrogen faster, suppress your weedy nitrogen fixers with newspaper covered by a few inches (approximately 7.5 cm) of aged compost as more stable carbon source. Then, plant nitrogen-fixing cover crops that are treated with rhizobia inoculant.

Crimson clover, Austrian peas, fava beans, and fenugreek are my favorites to use for this. Cover crop seed sellers usually offer the inoculant or can tell you the right kind to buy from other sellers.

Water plants well until they root well. Then mow these plants down just as they start to flower for maximum nitrogen capture. Repeat mowing until the plants stop regrowing. Wait a few weeks, then plant directly through the roots of the cover crops. That way, as the nitrogen decomposes it's already right there in your plant's root zone.

CLIMATE CONDITIONS

Understanding weeds and their niches within the context of your climate and soil conditions is also extremely important.

ARID SOIL ADEPTS

In arid climates, maintaining a constantly leafy and lush plant and robust microlife community isn't nature's goal. There's simply not enough regular rain flow to sustain that kind of foliage. Instead, there are usually a lot of moisture-triggered dormant seeds waiting just under that protective crust. There may also be roots that go dormant when dried but reanimate when wet. Plants with foliage that survive

dry spells or supply their own water needs, such as brushy evergreens and succulents, are also common in arid conditions.

As such, you may need to simulate a deep rain to really discover which weeds you'll need to control. Also, when you have lots of weeds specifically adapted to activate with water, part of your weed prevention plan will be to control where water and organic matter fall and flow. Otherwise, irrigation and soil improvement can be the cause of all sorts of weeds.

This is a perfect, though exaggerated, example of how taproots create water and organic matter slides in soil. The cavernous hole in the soil was a large chicory root (*Cichorium intybus*) that rotted. New plants are starting from living root portions.

WATER MOVERS

In places with seasonal or perpetually heavy rains, weeds also often explode to help move water out of soil to quickly prevent stagnation. Some plants act as umbrellas sheltering the soil. Weedy-type trees may grow taller faster to absorb and evaporate water away from the soil or redirect it using large leaves before it reaches the ground.

Fungi also frequent wet regions. They digest woody plant matter to increase moisture retention. Also, the fungal fruiting bodies of ground growing fungi are primarily made of water, which gets evaporated as they dry or consumed by critters. Mosses and lichens may also use and repel water to protect soil. Roots may buttress and channel water away from trees.

All of these are nature's solutions to high moisture levels in the soil. If you start ripping out these solutions without first finding new ways of moving water out of the garden, you could create your own drainage problems.

MIXED CLIMATE MASH-UPS

In climates with wet and dry periods, there will usually be a mix of targeted soil protecting plants that crop up like weeds in either situation. Those plants may also have seasonal preferences that coincide with the timing of those dry and wet periods.

Places with wet springs may have lots of cool season, early blooming, large-leaved plants that make use of cool spring rains and fewer daylight hours. If it gets hot and dry in summer, there may be an abundance of narrow-leaved annuals that secure the soil and take advantage of those sunny conditions. You could even have staggered germination so that you have multiple flushing of the same plants in some years and others that may only happen once.

In conditions like these, you may have to use both wet and dry climate control tactics in different parts of your garden and do more suppression in general.

ROOT STRUCTURE

Root structure can also tell you a lot about your weeds and the niches they are filling.

DEEP TAPROOTS

Many taprooted weed seeds have been designed to respond to moist organic matter sitting on top of hard soil. For example, they are often large and easily beaten into organic matter. But then they may require the seeds to stay in saturated soil for a few days to break down the heavy outer coating before germination. That ensures that taprooted plants grow when needed to move organic matter and moisture into soil.

Then, those tiny taproots use their piercing growing tips to dig down deep before filling like a balloon, using moisture and nutrients from up top. As they bore deeper underground, they also move moisture and organic matter deeper into the soil profile. Eventually, these roots die and decompose, creating a mine shaft that water and nutrients can freely flow into.

When drilling taproots, a prevalent weed in your soil, it's time to till naturally. Use the roots of trees, shrubs, and perennial plants in place of the weeds. Or sow ground-breaking cover crops like tillage radishes, mangels, and sweet potatoes. Don't harvest the roots. Instead, let them decompose in place to store carbon and water deeper underground where it's more stable.

Alternatively, just let the weeds do their good work. Many deep taproot-type weeds are biennial or short-lived perennials. They time out on their own after setting seeds. Of course, you don't want them to seed, so after they flower, cut off the heads as often as is necessary until they die.

BIOACCUMULATORS

Some taprooted plants also produce large quantities of vegetative leaf mass that decompose and provide necessary trace nutrients to shallower rooted plants. Thistles, docks, and comfrey are noted for this. In a sense, these plants are like elevators, getting minerals from down deep, then elevating up to the leaf level.

When you see these types of plants proliferating in your landscape, it's a good indication that your mineral bank in the topsoil is running low while your subsoil is well-stocked. Use those weeds as a cover crop. Just keep mowing them down and letting their own leaves smother them.

Also, consider planting some longer-living vegetative taprooted plants on purpose to fill this niche. For example, common milkweed (*Asclepias syriaca*)—beloved by monarch butterflies, unbothered by deer, and lovely to look at—uses its deep taproot, which can grow over 6 feet (1.8 m) per year, to thrive even in difficult conditions. It spreads by rhizomes and can become weedy, too. But it's easy to identify and keep contained by pulling new stems that come up.

Baptisia (*Baptisia* spp.) and butterfly weed (*Asclepias* spp.) are some other pollinator-friendly options with beneficial taproots that look beautiful in the garden. Many cultivars available today are beneficial to the soil and less likely to spread like weeds.

Sterile or Russian comfrey, also called Bocking 14 (*Symphytum* x *uplandicum*), is used by many organic gardeners as a trace mineral elevator. It can get enormous if you don't divide it regularly. But it's beautiful and extremely useful as a perennial green manure plant. It also doesn't spread invasively like other comfrey types do.

This looks like a fibrous root at first glance, but the root hairs all grow off the branched taproots rather than out of the crown the way fibrous roots would.

BRANCHING TAPROOTS

Some plants also start by growing a taproot. But when that root hits resistance in the soil or gets to a certain temperature level, it just stops growing. The crown of the plant may then start a new taproot that grows in a sideways direction instead.

Tall, top-heavy plants like trees and shrubs do this often. Then, once they have several anchoring taproots in place, the crown may switch over and create more fibrous roots from the crown.

These plants don't deepen the soil profile with their roots. Instead they build a fortress over it to keep other plants out. The roots of weeds with this habit often look like a hand grabbing up all the soil nutrients. Ragweed (*Ambrosia* spp.) is a perfect example of this. If you pull it out in dry weather, you'll often take a huge chunk of soil with the root mass because of all the thick taproots with hairy feeder roots growing from them.

The good news about these shallow-rooted, branched taproot-type weeds is that they are literally holding on for dear life because they didn't bother to root deeply. Mow them down, then block their access to light and water for a few weeks and they'll time out. Or repeatedly mow them until their season is over so they can't set seeds.

STORAGE TAPROOTS

Not all taproots look like daggers piercing the soil. Some fatten into round balls, oblong blocks, or other odd shapes. These specialized roots developed from genetic anomalies in their allele pairings that turned them from long taproots into top-heavy nutrient hoarders.

Cultivated beets, mangels, turnips, rutabaga, radish, carrots, parsnips, and sweet potatoes fall into this category. We don't generally call these plants weeds, but some of the heirloom types, started by seed, do still have a tendency toward delayed germination. I've had some seeds randomly germinate years after sowing. Control is easy, though—just harvest them for dinner.

The ancestors these plants diverged from have propensities to target certain kinds of minerals in the soil, like copper, zinc, manganese, and iron. As such, if weedy relatives of your favorite culinary roots try to take over certain parts of your garden, that can give you clues about what to plant next in your crop rotation.

If Palmer amaranth (*Amaranthus palmeri*) is having a field day in your bed, beets or mangels can fill that niche. Likewise, for garlic mustard (*Alliaria petiolate*) or any other wild mustard relatives, turnips, radish, or rutabaga might help. If wild carrots (*Daucus carota*), poison hemlock

Ragweed and milkweed intermingle against a backdrop of sunflowers.

(*Conium maculatum*), or any self-sowing herb with an umbel flower keep prettying up your plant patches, carrots and parsnips might be your next niche-filler. Sweet potatoes might also fill in for flowering morning glories if your soil is deep enough.

TUBERS, BULBS, CORMS, RHIZOMES, AND FATTENED STEMS

There are also some fibrous-rooted plants that get confused with taproots. These are the storage stems like tubers, bulbs, rhizomes, and other fattened stems. Potatoes (stem tubers), garlic and onions (stem bulbs), and ginger and turmeric (stem rhizomes) are some cultivated examples. The cultivated versions are easy to recognize and rarely get rated as weeds.

Nature, by contrast, makes storage stems that are designed primarily for making new plants, not storing food that's tasty to humans. Weedy rhizomes often look like slithering white snakes with thick, pointed heads that pierce sideways through soil. The bulbs or corms of weedy plants are smaller and more prolific than our larger cultivated kinds and may just look like clumps of dirt or rocks dangling from the roots.

Some weeds have both rhizomes and stem or root tubers, which makes them doubly good at surviving and spreading. Those tubers are also a reservoir of food and moisture that makes them able to thrive through tougher conditions than other plants. The beautiful but invasive orange day lilies (*Hemerocallis fulva*) that grow along roads in my area are a stunning example. Of course, so are dahlias. I sure wish they spread like weeds in my climate.

If you till weeds that have these underground rhizomes or storage stems, you just get lots more plants. The underground stem parts also have the capacity to survive in low-oxygen environments. Like mini-scuba divers with a small air tank, they can work their way up from thick mulch and grow around obstacles.

If these plants start spreading rapidly, these types of weeds usually indicate you have excess nutrients and moisture in your topsoil. If they're confined to a certain space, that might be a zone of accumulation where erosion is flowing into.

In my opinion, weedy rhizomatic or stem spreaders are the only weeds that warrant highly disruptive deep digging to thoroughly remove them. Tilling, mulching, smothering, or building beds over these rarely works long-term. They'll just use their mini air tanks to redirect

This section of rhizomes could become hundreds of new plants if not controlled quickly. Total eradication is the only answer for these weeds to prevent them from taking over your good garden soil.

around or move up into whatever nice space you are making. Total removal, or targeted confinement such as with underground impermeable barriers or trenching, and constant vigilance are usually required.

Japanese knotweed (*Polygonum cuspidatum*) is the most epic example of this class of weeds. It's even worked its way through stone masonry into the living areas in the UK. Kudzu (*Pueraria montana*) is a milder, but still nearly impossible to eradicate example of an invasive plant with both rhizomes and tubers for stem storage. Poison ivy (*Toxicodendron radicans*) is another invasive and painful stem spreader in this category. Thankfully, it spreads slower and is easier to manage than the first two examples (if you wear a hazmat suit).

These three weeds also aren't ideal for controlled burns. Above ground, they can provide fast-burning fuel. Below ground, those little scuba diving stems may survive burning and regenerate later.

Large stands of these weeds are often habitat for spiders, snakes, vermin, and other critters in their foliage. As such, suit-up in head-to-toe protection before you start clearing away the above-ground foliage. Mow down the above-ground stems using hedge trimmers and chainsaws. Gather up and remove the leaf matter as you go. These need to be bagged and delivered in person to the landfill for proper control.

Japanese knotweed (*Polygonum cuspidatum*) is very challenging to remove.

After top clearing is done, then comes the root excavation. In large areas, excavation equipment may be necessary. In smaller areas with less established root systems, shovels and digging bars may be sufficient.

Make sure you clear every bit of the root, rhizome, or tubers, or these plants will return. This is one time when you may want to dig up and loosen all the surrounding soil so you can sort through and pick out residual roots and stems.

 TOOL BAR

A digging bar is a heavy bar with a chiseled tip on one side and a small, flat tamper. You can use this to break up hard soil before digging with a shovel. It also makes a good lever to work under and lift out deep roots.

Digging bars come in different sizes and weights. Get one you can easily manage.

Even when you do a thorough job, you'll still need to monitor the area and remove survivors for many years. Before planting that area, you may want to grow cover crops or easy-to-grow annuals for a few years in case you need to dig for missed roots, rhizomes, or tubers again.

Once you are certain the weeds are gone, then plant perennials known to hold their own against running weeds. Lilac (*Syringa vulgaris*), coppiced willow (*Salix* spp.), fig (*Ficus carica*), hazelnut (*Corlus* spp.), and other shrubby plants with their own pervasive root systems are good options. These plants also need to be controlled with regular garden maintenance to make sure they don't spread. However, trimming suckers will keep them in check.

Poison Ivy Warning

Be cautious when handing poison ivy. It contains urushiol, a skin allergen, that can produce rashes and blisters. The urushiol can spread if you try to wipe it away. Use gloves to clean the affected area with a poison ivy treatment soap. Jewelweed (*Impatiens capensis*) sap, from crushed leaves and stems, is a natural antidote to urushiol. When rubbed on the affected, it may reduce inflammation and itching. Contact your doctor if serious blistering or other side effects occur.

WEED WHACK!

USE GOATS

If you have large areas of difficult-to-clear plants, goats might be an option. Before the goats arrive, any plants that should not be eaten are protected with various barriers. Then the goats are confined to the affected area using electric fencing. The goats are not fed any other feed sources to make sure they eat the weeds. Standard pet or dairy goats aren't used for clearing projects since they required a more varied diet and specific nutrients for long-term health.

Goats love certain weeds but are reluctant eaters of others. They must be really hungry to want most of the invasive weeds we'd like to get rid of in our landscapes.

These Jerusalem artichokes (*Helianthus tuberosus*) keep down weeds in the alley between my fruit trees, but can easily become a weed in some circumstances.

On a smaller scale, plants like nutsedge (*Cyperus* spp.), couch grass (*Elymus repens*), and dollarweed (*Hydrocotyle* spp.) are underground stem spreaders that can be challenging to control in organic vegetable gardens. They can grow right under the shallow root systems of most annual vegetables.

To control these, you also need to eradicate every bit of root or rhizome. In severe cases, you may need to take a few seasons off gardening in that area. Stop adding organic matter, dig out the underground stems, and don't water. Then, skip the water-retentive mulches and compost until the problem is solved. After that, grow dense stands of low-nutrient plants in that area for a while so you don't need to add more compost for fertility.

If these stem spreaders are lurking under established perennials where you can't dig, cover under and around the area with landscape fabric, weighted with rocks or bricks. Then control the plants that breech the perimeter until the parent plant eventually dies under the cover. This can take a few years.

No one likes the work involved in controlling these kind of stem spreaders. However, the conventional option is to use toxic herbicides repeatedly and continue fighting them with hand-pulling for years to come. Of course, those herbicides can also have lasting consequences for your garden.

Also, be cautious when bringing home any plants that spread by underground rhizomes, tubers, or fattened stems, unless you are certain they won't become invasive in your garden. For example, Jerusalem artichokes (*Helianthus tuberosus*), also called sunchokes, are hailed as an excellent perennial food vegetable. I grow them, cautiously, in certain areas of my landscape. But they aren't allowed near my vegetable garden.

Fibrous roots primarily grow directly from the crown, making them look like mops.

FIBROUS ROOTS

Finally, we come to the rest of the fibrous rooted plants. These come in all sorts of shapes and sizes, but for weed control purposes, I lump them into two categories.

Carpets

The carpets are the creeping spreaders. They spread by extending their thick, matted root system to cover a wider area. They also spread by stolons above ground, which allows them to crawl on soil and set new roots a short distance away. Unlike the rhizomatic creepers, carpet-like plants can be controlled using mulch or repeated mowing or addressing issues in the soil.

The carpets that love hot, dry, compacted conditions, such as crabgrasses (*Digitaria* spp.) and prostrate spurge (*Euphorbia humistrata*), indicate a need for more organic matter, regular watering, and some taprooted plants growing in that area. The kind that like moist, cool, fertile conditions, such as chickweed (*Stellaria media*) or speedwell (*Veronica* spp.), indicate open soil that needs a cover crop or ground cover.

Mops

Fibrous-rooted plants that look like a string mop in the soil but don't creep are the easiest to control. They often seed prolifically since they don't spread easily by other methods. Horseweed (*Conyza canadensis*), Jimsonweed (*Datura stramonium*), and lespedeza (*Kummerowia striata*, syn. *Lespedeza striata*) are some that I let grow and then mow before they seed.

These are often open soil opportunists that just indicate you ought to be growing more plants to take up that space.

Carbon Fixation Methods

Carbon fixation is another increasingly important way to categorize weeds and the role they fill in your landscape. Carbon fixation is the process by which plants convert inorganic carbon, primarily carbon dioxide, into plant-usable organic carbon. The main methods plants use are referred to as C3, C4, and CAM. Those short names relate to the chemical pathways plants use to separate carbon molecules from air and sequester them during photosynthesis.

C3 CARBON FIXERS

C3 carbon-fixing plants, which include about 85 percent of all plants and most garden plants, collect carbon in the least efficient way of the three fixation types. They leave their stomata (pores on plant leaves) open all the time. In moderate weather, this is no problem. It's like having the windows open to allow fresh air exchange. In wet conditions, this is also useful because it pulls moisture out of the soil and releases it back into the air, reducing the risks of soil becoming boggy.

Unfortunately, in hot, dry weather, keeping stomata open is like standing on scorching asphalt instead of going in the shade. It results in plants overheating and using a lot of water to cool themselves. When the soil runs out of available water, the plant begins using up the water reserves in its roots and leaves. Crispy leaf tips are a surefire sign plants ran out of water.

There are some C3 plants that can tolerate hotter temperatures and drier conditions because they have other adaptations (not related to carbon fixation) that increase their heat tolerance. Plus, soil and its water-holding capacity also play an enormous role in how long C3 plants can thrive outside their comfort zone. Overall, though, C3 carbon-fixing plants thrive in cooler temperatures (55 to 75°F [13 to 24°C]) when soil is better able to hold moisture and with consistent watering.

This is one of the main reasons why, around midsummer, gardeners—especially vegetable gardeners—start to feel overwhelmed by weeds. We're usually not watering enough for our C3 plants in these warmer conditions. We'll cover ways to dramatically increase the water-holding capacity in your soil in Part 2. In the meantime, though, to keep weeds from overrunning your C3 plants in hot or dry weather, consider these tools.

TOOL BAR

Soaker hoses allow water to seep slowly into the soil.

SOAKER HOSE

A soaker hose is shaped like a normal garden hose, but it seeps water along its entire length. To use, drag your regular hose adjacent to the area you want to water. Then attach the soaker hose and lay it across the dry area. You can run it in an "S" configuration or a straight line to cover your area.

Soaker hoses rely on water pressure to operate. The outdoor hose spigot in a modern house on city water can usually support a 100-foot (30 m) soaker hose. But if you have lower than average water pressure, you may want to start with 25 feet (8 m) and see how that goes.

Soaker hoses are the best way to get water deep into soil without hand-watering. Leave them on long enough to penetrate below the top couple of inches (approximate 5 cm) into the subsoil.

They are prone to clogging, can be expensive to replace, and can't be run over long distances. For larger areas or for water sources with slightly larger particulate matter, drip tape or drip line are possible options.

DRIP LINE/TAPE

Drip line or drip tape function similarly, except the tape is wide and flat and the line is a narrow tube. Drip line lasts longer but costs more. The line can come with water emitters preinstalled at regular intervals. Alternatively, it can come as a solid line that you punch the emitters into around plants that need water. Drip tape comes prepunched with holes at regular distances.

For small areas, start with inexpensive kits from your garden center. For larger areas, irrigation supply retailers should be able to help you figure out what supplies you need and how to configure your lines to ensure you have adequate water pressure over the entire line.

WEED WHACK!

WATERING CAN MATH FOR THE VEGETABLE GARDEN

I'm still partial to watering cans because I control and calculate the flow. Every 0.6 gallons (2.3 L) of water poured on a square foot (.09 square m) of soil simulates about 1 inch (2.5 cm) of rain. Now, the rule about needing 1 inch (2.5 cm) of rain a week is not accurate for most gardens. (We'll get more into why it's not in Part 2). However, it's fun to calculate how many gallons your beds need to get a sense of how many inches per rain really will be sufficient for your plants.

THE OLLA SOLUTION

In small gardens, an elegant low-tech option is to use an olla to deliver water deeper into soil. Ollas are terra-cotta containers dug into the soil and filled with water. When your soil is moist, the water level will remain stable in the olla, not draining into the soil. As your soil dries, though, the water seeps through the pores of the terra-cotta and is wicked up by the soil.

This sounds like magic, but it's the same basic concept your skin and stomach run on. Water wants to equalize with its surroundings. So, when the olla is wet and the soil is dry, the water wants to move into the soil and the porosity of the terra-cotta allows that to happen.

OLLA HOW-TO

You can buy olla pots that have large bulbous water receptacles buried under ground attached to pipelike tubes for filling them. They're lovely but quite costly. They also need to be removed before the ground freezes in cold areas to prevent breaking.

As an alternative for easy removal and to save some money, you can also make your own DIY ollas using terra-cotta pots from your local garden center. Because they don't have the long neck and aren't buried as deeply in the ground, they are easier to remove for winter care. The downside is the water evaporates faster, so you need to fill these DIY ollas more often. Also, they take up more space at the surface of the soil than the narrow-necked version does.

Still, they are a wonderful tool to cool and satiate thirsty C3 plants. Start with a few in your vegetable or flower areas to see how you like them. Here's any easy way to make them at home.

You need a terra-cotta pot, saucer, and putty to make the olla. Optional: A bucket is useful for holding the soil you dig out and the watering can is handy to later fill the olla.

1 Pick up a terra-cotta pot with a saucer from your local garden store.

2 Dig the pot into the ground. Use your spade or shovel to mark the area in your soil. Then remove the soil to the depth of the pot. Backfill around the pot to secure it in place. It needs full contact with soil for that wicking action to work.

3 Find something to block the hole at the bottom. A trick I learned from Tanya Anderson, author of *A Woman's Garden*, is to cover the hole with mounting putty (available at most hardware stores). That way, you can remove it later if you want. However, any non-toxic water resistant putty product will also work.

4 Fill the pot with water and put the saucer lid on upside down as a cover to reduce evaporation.

5 Fill as often as is necessary to keep it full.

6 In cold climates, before freezing temperatures, remove the olla and put a plastic pot filled with soil in its place to keep the hole filled through winter. In spring, put the olla back in the place of the plastic pot.

Ollas work great for perennial plant areas and vegetable beds. If you sow seeds around your olla, you'll still want to top water the seeded area until the seedling roots grow into the olla watering zone.

STEP
2

Dig the olla into the soil.

STEP
3

Seal the drainage hole with putty.

CAM CARBON FIXERS

Crassulacean acid metabolism (CAM) plants do their carbon capture by day when its sunny and warm. But they release their unwanted oxygen at night. That means their stomata open only at night when the air is usually cooler. This carbon-fixing adaptation ensures they don't overheat as easily as C3 plants in hot weather. CAM plants still require water for their processes, but since they stay cooler by day, they use a lot less water than C3 plants do.

CAM plants are less common in most gardens than C3 plants. However, if you live in a desert climate, you are likely growing some. Many—though not all—cacti, agave, stonecrops, euphorbias, and even some lilies and grape-related vining plants have CAM carbon fixation. Some epiphytes (orchids) or bromeliads (pineapple) also use this method, though they also require more humidity to thrive.

A few CAM plants have become weedy, such as Spanish moss (*Tillandsia usneoides*). Although this bromeliad (which isn't from Spain, or from the moss family) doesn't usually kill its host, it can shade out lower branches and cause parts of the tree to die. Despite that minor limb loss, Spanish moss is one of nature's go-to plants for providing shade for trees that might otherwise overheat from C3 carbon fixation.

Common purslane (*Portulaca oleracea*) is generally considered a C4 plant. But it also has what's called CAM plasticity. That means that under stress, if C4 methods aren't sufficient for plant survival, it can also use CAM carbon-fixing processes. Wood sorrel (*Oxalis* spp.) may also be developing more CAM plasticity. In fact, many more plants are expected to exhibit CAM plasticity in the future. It's emerging as another potential tool nature uses to make some plants more resilient on a warming planet.

Most CAM plants tend to be problem solvers. They generally don't need to be controlled. But if you use them in your landscape, try to locate them in areas that are cooler by night during hot weather to make carbon fixation less water intensive.

C4 CARBON FIXERS

C4 carbon-fixing weeds make the fiercest weed foes in warm weather. They've evolved a carbon fixation process that doesn't require much water. They also have more control over when they open their stomata. They can close them in hot weather to preserve moisture. But they can also leave them open all the time in moderate weather to fix more carbon in a hurry.

Effectively, these C4 plants are living off-grid in passive solar comfort during hot weather, while C3 plants are burning up trying to stay cool. Yet, C4s also live on-grid in good weather to take advantage of the best of both worlds.

C4 plants also make lower quality leaves that don't take as many plant resources as C3 plants. This allows them to spend that extra energy making deeper and more extensive root networks, giving them another competitive advantage over C3 plants when it comes to nutrient and water access. As such, these plants tend to be nutrient hogs in our vegetable gardens in summer.

If C4 weeds are the only ones growing well in your landscape, consider growing C4 plants on purpose until you've done the deeper soil work we'll cover in Parts 2 and 3.

This is a very nonscientific, big picture look at carbon fixation methods. It's meant to lay the groundwork to help you create your own personalized weed prevention plan. Lots of new research about carbon fixation is emerging regularly. My personal hope is that one day we'll go the garden center and find the carbon fixation data listed on the label. But even with just this introduction, you can begin to use these plant types to make smart strategic decisions for weed prevention in your garden.

For example, in places where you have no or low weed tolerance, you need to stay on top of C4 weeds by giving your C3 and CAM plants ideal care. Interplant to shade out C4 seedlings. Mulch to suppress germination. Disrupt seedlings before it gets hot. But in areas where you aren't actively gardening yet, why not let C4 weeds do their good work and start adding carbon to your soil?

C4 grasses can easily overtake garden beds or planter boxes in hot, dry months if they are not controlled. Good watering, early weeding, and keeping those spaces heavily planted will help.

Parasitic Weeds

Unlike the beneficial CAM Spanish moss, there are some parasitic weeds that essentially usurp the carbon fixation powers of other plants. Field dodder (*Cuscuta campestris*) looks like silly string but is definitely no joke when it comes to killing other plants. Since it doesn't have its own chlorophyll, it can't photosynthesize on its own. Instead, it taps into other plants' stems and steals their processed carbon.

Likewise, dwarf mistletoes like *Arceuthobium vaginatum* that lack chlorophyll grow best on trees with enhanced carbon fixation, such as in thinned forests with plenty of water. Parasitic misletoes, referred to as true or leafy mistetoes, like *Phoradendron leucarpum*, by contrast, only take water and minerals from their host trees. They can do their own carbon fixation by the C3 method. There are also other types of mistletoe that grow on CAM and C3 *Mimosaceae* species that both take and make their own carbon.

In all cases, once these parasitic weeds have sunk their teeth-like haustoria roots into your plants, your best bet is to remove the affected area or remove the entire plant to prevent spreading to other host plants.

WEED WHACK!

INTERPLANTING OR LAYERED PLANTING

Another way to create beauty and help keep C3 plants from losing their cool when it gets hot is to use close groupings of compatible plants to create a cooling microclimate. It's kind of like creating a mini-forest in your landscape.

Combining C3 and some well-behaved C4 plants of various heights, root types, and light needs closely together can help trap cool moisture closer to plants and reduce the risk of heat stress. In vegetable gardening, we call this interplanting or intercropping. In ornamental gardening or edible landscaping, we often call it layering or guilding. When used effectively, plants stay cool and weeds are shaded with close, well-planned groupings.

That three sisters grouping I gave in the introduction is a simple example of interplanting to keep soil cool and preserve moisture. The corn is a C4 plant that will use less water to fix carbon, leaving more behind for the C3 squash and beans. However, the squash also shades the roots for all three plants, which reduces water loss by evaporation so there's more for everyone.

When interplanting in close groupings, you also want to ensure that there is sufficient soil life and nutrients to support all the plants. Normally, corn will aggressively outcompete other plants to get nitrogen in hot weather. In this mix, though, that's not a problem because beans fix their own nitrogen in collaboration with those rhizobia bacteria. Meanwhile, the squash should be planted on nutrient rich mounds to retain water and keep the corn from hogging the soil nutrients. Plus, the close grouping keeps all three plants cooler so corn doesn't get to use its C4 advantage as competitively.

It takes some research and experimentation to find the right plant groupings to create a supportive system that preserves moisture, shades out weeds, and nourishes all parties without becoming competitive.

Seasonality

Carbon fixation is tied loosely to seasonality. For example, C3 plants like cool weather. CAM prefer hot days/cool night plants. Those C4s like it hot. But those preferences only relate to when the plants are most likely to do the brunt of their carbon fixing and growing. They don't always correlate to when those plants germinate or leaf out.

Many cool season weeds germinate in warm temperatures, such as in late summer. Then, when you first notice them in late winter or early spring, they're already well-established. Many hot weather plants start as soon as the soil warms up in spring and even have light frost tolerance.

Don't wait for weeds to become large to start your disturbance. Identify your mature weeds during their prime growing season. Then, find out what temperatures they germinate at and what their seedlings look like, so you can control them early.

You can also target your weed control tactics using knowledge about the seasonal niche your weeds fill. For example, cool season weeds that are naturally stressed by hot weather are often easy to control with heat-based treatments.

This cool weather-loving Persian speedwell (*Veronica persica*) is giving a fall-started curly dock a little competition.

WEED WHACK!

BOILING WATER

Pouring boiling water on cool season plants is killer. Like, literally. Just make sure to do it when soil or surfaces are already warm. Also, boiling water to pour on a couple of weeds is a waste of resources. Pull those by hand and burn calories instead. But if you overfilled your tea kettle, apply it to weeds on your sun-warmed paths, patios, driveways, and sidewalk cracks as a test.

For persistent perennial C3 plants, get out your mega-pot to heat over a camp stove next to the weedy area. When the water boils, use a smaller pot as a dipping ladle to pour scalding water all around the root zone. Wait a few minutes, then repeat, until the plant appears painfully distressed. Then, mow down the plant to the soil level and cover with cardboard and compost to heal the scorched earth.

I use hot beds in my greenhouse to warm seedlings from below. But they work very well outdoors on cool season weeds, too.

HOT BEDS AND LASAGNA GARDENING

Hot beds are a great way to get a head start on the planting season while neutralizing cool season weeds. Farmers used to make a large pile of barn litter (manure, hay, straw, and urine) with just the right carbon-to-nitrogen ratio to start a thermophilic (hot) compost pile. The heat from the pile killed off cool season weeds and prevented new seeds from germinating. It also warmed the soil below, waking up beneficial bacteria earlier than usual. Then, leachate (runoff) from the compost bed offered a high-nutrient treat that set off a bacteria-breeding frenzy.

After the thermophilic pile ran its course and began to cool down, the newly expanded bacteria below were already hard at work integrating all that leftover carbon and nutrients into the soil for the growing season. Within a couple of months, the massive pile became a slightly mounded weed-free planting bed.

Historically, farmers then used those beds to plant cool season root vegetables. Today, though, we know that foodborne pathogens from manure need more like six months of aging after composting for safety. As such, hot beds are perfect for early season cover crops, followed by mid-season vegetables with a late-season harvest today. If you don't have barn litter, just build a normal compost pile, but use some extra high nitrogen materials to ensure the pile runs hot in cold weather.

 ## TOOL BAR

THE FLAME WEEDER

Another perfect tool for heating up cool season weeds is a flame weeder. This is a propane torch used to scald root systems and dry out plants. The torch is purchased separately, then connected to a propane tank. Those tanks can be heavy. So, some torches come attached to a dolly.

Make sure there are no burn prohibitions in your area and have a fire extinguisher or hose handy. Plus, be ready to call the fire department just in case. Then follow the directions that come with your torch.

The general goal is not to catch the plant on fire. Burning foliage often results in the plant growing back more vigorously.

The flame weeder works great on cool season annuals. But I rarely need it because most of my cool season weeds are edible for me or my chickens.

Instead, heat the soil around the root zone and stress plants to death by making it feel like the Sahara for a while. Flame weeding is even more effective right after cool season plants flower.

These smartweed seedlings germinated around March 7th and waited until late April to put out their first leaves. They survived three hard frosts. By mid-May they'd covered a 4 x 8-foot (1.2 x 2.4-m) area.

WARM-SEASON WEEDS

I could offer you countless examples of warm-season weeds. But you probably already have a long list in mind. These are the weeds that show up exactly when our cool season C3 plants are finally sizing up, starting to flower, and the garden is about to be magazine cover stunning. Then—whoosh!—weeds spread like wildfire through the garden.

The thing is, they didn't just show up the moment it got hot. They were most likely there for weeks before you noticed them because they often start in cooler temperatures than we expect. For example, smartweed (*Persicaria pensylvanica*, syn. *Polygonum pensylvanicum*) is a warm season weed that germinates months before it starts actively growing above ground. Then, one warm day, spreading stems and leaves explode from unexpectedly developed root systems. Those roots also intentionally entangle themselves in the roots of other plants to complicate controlling by pulling.

Despite their sneaky cool season start, though, warm-season weeds do have a weakness for sunlight. That's why so many of them spread out or creep to broaden their sun reach.

WEED WHACK!

THROW SHADE

Want to slow down those sun lovers? Throw some shade on their parade. Especially if you can catch them just as they start their growth spurt, shade can keep them in check until you can control them more completely.

It may not be attractive, but these are the plants that will be most bothered if covered by old carpet, plastic sheeting, or cardboard under a potted plant. Anything you've got that robs them of sunlight as they start to grow will slow their spread.

The invasive Japanese stiltgrass (*Microstegium vimineum*) had admirable abilities to suppress other weeds. Only an existing taprooted plant made it through last year's thick root-thatching.

THE ULTIMATE WEED-FREE WEED

There aren't many warm-season plants that won't be daunted by light deprivation. Unfortunately, one that's becoming a persistent weed in many parts of the United States is Japanese stiltgrass (*Microstegium vimineum*). Not only does it grow quite well in full shade, but it's also a C4 carbon fixer. Its biggest secret weapon, though, is thatching.

It's an annual that grows up to 3 feet (1 m) tall with feathery grass leaves atop shallow, heavily matted root systems. It seeds profusely on top of its own root system in mid-to late summer. Then those tops fall over to protect and mulch the seeds below. Like a thatched roof, the roots and leaf cover reduce water flow from reaching the soil. That, in turn, prevents seeds in the soil bank below from germinating. Then, when the warmth and light conditions are right, the stiltgrass seeds germinates and grow right through last year's root mass.

This plant is literally an expert at preventing other weeds. I have a lot of admiration for this plant, but little tolerance for it in my garden. Keep your soil planted year-round and it will have a hard time getting started. Also, this warm-season weed will take a hint from a flame weeder. That dense, matted root system forsakes depth for density, making it prone to drying out faster than other C4 weeds. Also, repeated mowing and raking out of old growth to remove the thatching benefits, then sowing an aggressive cover crop replacement will help.

Now, there is one last weed-prone garden situation we have to cover before we get to move on to your test and homework.

Monoculture

The word *monoculture* only dates back about 120 years. It describes the agricultural technique of growing one crop at high density to allow for easier harvests and care. It applies to field crops like corn, wheat, and soybeans. It's also used for managed pine forests or large plant nurseries that grow multiples of the same plant grouped together.

Frankly, nature doesn't understand monoculture. It's just too risky. If some pest, pathogen, or weather condition takes out that single crop, then soil and all the natural systems like water filtration, air purifying, wildlife support, and more would suffer. The broad range of possible environmental factors—such as heat, cold, drought, deluge, pests, pathogens, wildlife fluctuations, and more—make plant diversity a better strategy to ensure the stability of natural systems. That's why nature has so many weeds and ways of spreading weeds available as a resource.

Sometimes, we create monocultures for aesthetic reasons. But I have to warn you: that's not weed-free gardening. That's weed-encouraging gardening and you should expect to do a lot of work to maintain monocultures. The most common example of a monoculture in home gardens is the grass lawn. It's also one of the hardest places to keep weed-free without herbicides.

Practicing Weed Prevention

Now that you have a good background in deep thinking about weed prevention, you're more prepared than most gardeners to choose the right kind of preventative controls and interventions to transition to weed-free gardening.

Just keep in mind, the strategies you use for the vegetable garden will be completely different than for a lawn, a food forest, or your pollinator-friendly wildflower patch. Your choices will also be dependent on the style of your garden, your climate, and what you hope to grow. The weeds you are dealing with, the extent of their spread, and your patience for problem solving also need to play a role in which strategies you choose.

Your path to peace in the garden is personal and should be a reflection of the plants and design ideas you love. But it will be a shorter path if you get to know your landscape and its needs intimately, using your weeds as your guide.

Now, for a little homework before you move on to Part 2.

In this low-maintenance path, dense plantings of mint, goldenrod, sunchokes, and perennial flowers crowd out weeds along the sides while the compacted, high-traffic center impedes their growth. Though easy to maintain, this aesthetic is not ideal for all gardens.

This park-like area of my front yard is a work in progress. Weeds are at work doing regenerative soil work, but I've also incorporated in some edibles like apple, hazelnuts, and catmint.

To Do! Get to Know Your Landscape

Just in case you aren't well-versed in garden planning and design, I want to point out that creating or changing your garden is not a low-risk activity. If you dig without knowing where your power lines are, put a garden in a poorly drained location, correct drainage issues without understanding the basics of landscape hydrology, add rain barrels before calculating and directing overflow, terrace without understanding your soil, compost in a new location without evaluating the site first, etc., calamity can ensue.

That's why being able to read your landscape and knowing the basics of garden design are skills that need to come early in your progression as a gardener. So, if this is your first gardening book or you're scaling up from having a small bed to a full-blown garden, take some time getting to know your landscape topography and environmental conditions intimately.

Following is a list of some of what you'll need to know before you make changes to your landscape. It's in ranked order based on the things that are hardest to control or work around leading up to things you can address with your garden design plan.

1. Natural Factors

Natural factors are pretty much out of your control. It's easier to understand and work with these conditions than try to change them. Cold or heat hardiness zones are important for identifying the range of plants that can survive your climate. Intensity of storms, frequency of rains during your growing season, humidity ranges, chill hours, wind patterns, sun and shade patterns, and day length throughout the year also play a big role in plant selection, placement, and care.

2. Regulatory Concerns

Legal codes can limit your gardening choices. Knowing the exact location of utility lines and access points, easement areas, property lines, septic tanks, drainage and water pipes, and more are mandatory before making landscape changes. Also, consider how these changes will impact your neighbors to avoid potential problems down the road.

3. Resources and Challenges

Every landscape has available resources and challenges. The hose spigot on your house is a resource since it makes watering easier. Electrical access can be valuable, too. Neighbors who like to spray herbicide along their fence line create weed-free challenges. Wildlife activity, pets, kids, and other users of your property can also be resources or challenges depending on your dreams for your garden. Anything that can make weed-free gardening easier or harder needs to be assessed and factored into your decisions.

4. Layout

The slope of your land, zones of water accumulation or runoff, microclimates, sun/shade profiles, fences, outbuildings, aboveground and underground obstacles, and more will influence the kind of decisions you make in your weed-free garden. Some of this can be worked around. But it's usually easier to embrace your existing conditions than try to change them radically.

5. Soil Type

Your soil type, drainage, moisture retention, nutrient composition, pH, organic matter content, areas of compaction, and more all play a role in what will grow where you live. Professional soil tests can offer insights. But sometimes it's more fun and insightful to figure this out on your own.

The Internet is full of fun experiments you can do to get to know your soil better. Mason jar soil type tests, cabbage alkalinity tests, baking soda tests, worm counts, and more can all bring you greater familiarity with your soil. Stephania Rose, the founder of the gorgeous website Garden Therapy, authored a lovely book, *Garden Alchemy*, that's a wonderful one-stop resource for DIY garden tests and soil amendments.

Soil ranks last on the list, though, because organic gardening is all about improving soil. We're going to get into deep details on how to improve it quickly and effectively in Parts 2 and 3.

I call this the turd test, because it makes kids laugh. But if you can make your soil look like this, I guarantee you've got heavy clay.

Do your journaling in the garden to make it more pleasurable. Almost any garden can fit a small table and a chair or two if you plan it right.

To Do! Keep a Garden Journal

I also encourage you to keep detailed garden notebooks or take photo journals so you can keep track of trends in your garden. Most of us can't rely on our memories for this because they are only partly accurate. In fact, many experts believe our subconscious alters memories on purpose to make them more useful in keeping us safe in the future.

So, a small patch of sow thistle (*Sonchus oleraceus*) might morph into "it took over the garden" in our memories. Yet, since sow thistle is an indicator of abundant nutrients and open, full sun space in your garden, it probably didn't overwhelm existing plants entirely. Also, if you cooked that sow thistle up like spinach, you might think there were only two plants, not the twenty you ate.

As you get to know your garden and get into the habit of journaling about it, focus on detailed facts. Note weather events, when plants flower, new weed eruptions, successes, failures, things you tried in the garden, and ideas you have for the future. Also, feel free throw in some philosophizing and flowery musings, too.

NATURE—THE ORIGINAL DISRUPTER

Recently in the Eastern United States, billions of periodical seventeen-year cicadas burrowed from up several feet below ground to molt, eat the sap of plants, mate, lay eggs in the stems of trees and shrubs, and then die. Their newly hatched nymphs then fed and did further damage to their host plant before falling to the ground. There, they burrowed back down to feed on plant roots for seventeen years before the cycle starts again.

The fact that there can be as many as 2 million of these large insects per acre in the regions they inhabit is impressive to most people. However, for me it's their incredible environmental impact that really fascinates.

PERIODIC CICADAS

Cicada escape tunnels are about the width of the tip of a wine cork and have the beneficial effect of naturally aerating the soil. In fact, they can be so prolific that it looks like someone ran over the area with a lawn aerator. Those tunnels also disturb and expose dormant seeds stored deep in the soil, causing weed explosions. Most of the plants are the soil healing short-lived biomass makers that benefit the soil. But they also leave a legacy of new seeds on the surface of soil to sow again soon if not controlled early.

Also, as the exoskeletons and carcasses of cicadas decay, they provide a huge nutrient boost to the soil. The result is a huge flush of new growth from the same plants they nearly decimated with their mating cycle. Of course, that kind of nutrient spike at the soil's surface also contributes to huge amounts of new weeds, in addition to those that came up with the cicadas breaking ground.

Studies also show that the bird populations increase thanks to the highly nutritious and abundant cicada swarms that feed them. And since birds aren't feeding on caterpillars as much during cicada mating season, many of those populations regenerate, too. Then come the moles! Though moles only breed once a year, the extent of their excavation in search of cicadas is massive compared to other years. Also, the glut of cicadas means digging predators aren't as hungry for moles, so more mole pups make it to maturity, compounding the increased mole activity.

Moles are absolutely wonderful eaters of prolific grubs that could otherwise become pests in your garden. For example, on my homestead, they are the top predator for the grubs of the invasive, leaf-munching, orgy-having Japanese beetles (*Popillia japonica Newman*). They also eat earthworms that, frankly, can get out of hand in a compost- and mulch-rich garden. Plus, they naturally break up compaction and rejuvenate matted root systems with their digging habits. Like most critters, though, they were so fat from cicada larva that more grubs matured and mated to make more grubs.

On the downside, short-term plant damage is extensive. Weed pressure is intense. The sound, smell, and sheer numbers of insect and mole hills in your soft garden soil make these cyclical cicadas feel like a plague. Overall, though, as a nature lover, I assure you this amazing event adds up to a net gain with enormous regenerative benefits to natural ecosystems.

If you mowed more often as weeds came up, all those nutrients could just be an incredible boon to your organic garden. Yet, in my case, I wasn't expecting the periodical cicadas when they hit. I'd lived through Brood X (one of the seventeen different populations of seventeen-year cicadas) in Maryland in 2004, but I didn't realize there were multiple broods. So, I was shocked when Brood IX came up a year earlier in 2020 in my North Carolina garden when I hadn't planned any extra time in my schedule to keep up with the mowing.

That was a valuable reminder of how important it is to check with your forestry service, agricultural office, or life long gardeners near you to find out what

Caught in the act, this romantic couple isn't at risk for swarming. They're just your ordinary garden-variety grasshoppers enjoying really (re)productive time on my red perilla.

cyclical wildlife patterns need to be factored into your weed-free garden plans.

Only some parts of the United States have periodical cicadas. But other insects, such as Lepidoptera (butterfly family), Heteroptera (true bugs), Homoptera (beetles), and Diptera (flies), cause periodic disturbances, too. Then, of course, there are plagues of locusts in desert regions.

Locusts are grasshoppers renamed when they start to swarm. This happens when heavy rains during breeding season encourage excessive egg laying in moist soil. Then, the large food supply, also due to the heavy rain, triggers all those extra, normally solitary grasshoppers to eat foods that alter their physical appearance. They suddenly become gregarious and band together like, well, a plague of locusts.

On the surface this seems like it benefits grasshopper populations and not much else. Personally, though, I believe something deeper is at work here. All those plants, triggered into action by the rain, grew rapidly, drawing the water out of the ground and preventing erosion. Then, before the plants can dry out the desert soil entirely, hordes of grasshoppers eat the plants to the ground, leaving the roots intact to protect the soil. It's almost as if nature used the grasshoppers to mow down unwanted weeds just like we do in our gardens.

As with the cicadas, locusts are part of a much bigger natural picture than just the disturbance they cause to foliage. Of course, knowing that doesn't make it any easier for the folks who suffer so much devastation to agricultural crops. Understanding cycles like heavy rainfall leading to plagues of locusts, though, can help us figure out when and how best to protect our gardens from predictable natural events.

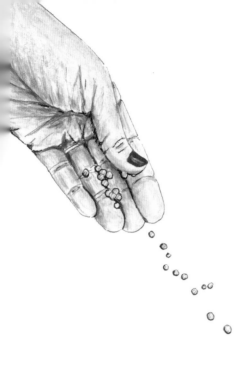

PART TWO

MAINTENANCE

Today, alleviating symptoms has become the standard for self-care in many busy lives. If we're tired, we drink coffee. If a tension headache takes over, we take pills. If we feel generally icky, we take vitamins. More sleep, less stress, and a healthier lifestyle would be more durable answers. But they can be hard to come by.

That symptom-alleviating approach carries into our garden care, too. We reach for nitrogen if plants seem sluggish. We add phosphorus if plants aren't blooming vigorously enough. We kill weeds or insects if plants aren't defending themselves sufficiently against those attacks. Unfortunately, those temporary remedies only invite weeds to thrive in our gardens.

Water-soluble nitrogen gets snatched up by aggressive weeds. Extra phosphorous interferes with cultivated plant absorption of iron and zinc, resulting in shallow-rooted weed-prone plants. Even narrowly targeted products disturb the microbiome in the soil just as antibiotics for an infection upset human gut health and digestion. Every quick fix can create challenges in our soil that weeds arrive to correct.

Additionally, most of the inexpensive products available to gardeners were developed for industrial farms. They get packaged in smaller quantities or diluted formulas for home use. Yet, when professionals use those tools, they do so in conjunction with soil tests and plant tissue samples. They perform cost/benefit analysis, review past herbicide use records, and keep up with continuing education. Home gardeners, by contrast, often apply these same highly specialized products without reading the multipage instruction labels offered to compensate for a lack of agricultural training. We pay and spray with the misplaced trust that because it's in the garden center it can't be that bad. The result is that significant amounts of toxic chemical runoff come from home landscapes and weeds become rampant.

"Temporary remedies only invite weeds to thrive."

Organic gardeners aren't always better. Some organic methods, used without careful consideration, can have unintended toxic consequences, too. Think about this for a minute.

Does nature routinely mound up chicken manure, coffee grounds, herbicide-laced banana peels, strawberry tops, and outer leaves of vegetable heads so high that they heat to over 135°F (57°C)?

Nature adds organic matter in small amounts over time—bird poop here, leaf matter there, a calcium-rich snail shell over there. Larger amounts, such as fall leaf drop, are carbon-rich "browns" that decompose slowly when not mixed with nitrogen-rich "greens," like in our compost piles. They also come down in cool weather as another fail-safe to prevent hot composting.

Sometimes, natural events can trigger rapid decomposition. For example, after a flood recedes, accumulations of dead life-forms will rot or get hot. Yet, this is an emergency response to a cataclysmic event. Then, nature follows up with a dizzying array of plants to work those excess nutrients back into the soil.

In nature, compost is damage control. Basically, that's its purpose in our gardens, too. But just like in nature, using freshly made compost in our gardens will trigger the same dizzying array of plants to work those nutrients into the soil. Plus, making compost produces biochemical oxygen demand (BOD) and phenols and leachate runoff that are temporarily detrimental to soil life and dangerous for fresh water supplies. It also increases weeds in the area where the compost is made.

Choosing the right mulch and addressing drainage around beds is critical for good soil maintenance.

Another DIY garden fix is baking soda, a.k.a. sodium bicarbonate. When mixed with horticultural oil and applied topically, it has some usefulness for certain plants as a fungicide against powdery mildew and black spot. Some gardeners also use it use as a fertilizer for tomatoes. Unfortunately, the sodium in baking soda is the same basic stuff that's in sodium chloride, a.k.a. salt.

Do you remember when I mentioned the Romans sowed salt into fields as a broad-spectrum herbicide? Overuse of baking soda, or any sodium-containing soil amendment, is another good way to sow the seeds of your own demise. Many weeds thrive in sodium-rich soil, whereas cultivated plants often can't.

The fact is, most of our landscape soil is in a state of emergency. So, we must use amendments and tools that are likely to cause weeds in the short-term to have a healthier garden in the long-term. However, any short-term fix that doesn't contribute to better long-term health needs to be banned in weed-free gardening.

Soil

In any garden that you harvest from regularly, resupplying the soil nutrients using compost is critical. Otherwise, soil will just become depleted, and even more weeds will come to heal it. But you can make piles safer by controlling the decomposition rates and siting them where leachate can't run off or down into waterways. Plus, aging compost makes it safer and more beneficial in planting areas.

Baking soda may be a good emergency option if safer options like potassium bicarbonate aren't available (e.g., pandemic gardening). In general, though, anything that's laced with sodium ought to come with a long-term weed-maker warning.

I share these examples because I want to make clear that weed-free gardening isn't a gardening instruction set to follow or a product to apply. It's a mind-set wherein you think more holistically about your garden as a natural system. In that system, there are no quick fixes—even organic ones—that won't automatically trigger ripple effects in your garden.

Also, in weed-free gardening, prevention and maintenance aren't two separate things. They're more like your brain and your body. Prevention is the thought process. Maintenance is the physical action you take in the garden. And soil is the heart of this whole system.

So, let's take a deep dive into what soil is and how we can take action to heal it while minimizing the risk for weed invasions.

The basic definition of soil is that it is made up of organic matter (leaf debris, compost, decaying critters, roots), inorganic matter (rocks, clay, sand, minerals), air, water, and microscopic and macroscopic life-forms. But I want to add one more dimension to the definition of soil for weed-free gardening.

Soil is a dynamic, complex, and responsive system designed by nature wherein all the elements (organic matter, water, air, inorganic matter, and life-forms) collaborate, compete, and coexist in ways that are mostly automated.

When you view Earth from outer space, it looks like a big ball of beautiful colors. You don't realize the immensity and complexity of all the human activity down below. Our vantage point on soil is the same. We're simply too far away, relative to the size of most of the things that exist in soil, to see all the incredible activities happening there.

Nonetheless, soil is full of beings working in their own ways to produce, consume, store, and share products and information. These life-forms also reproduce, move around to varying degrees, respond to changes in their environment, and eventually die just like we do. There are obvious differences between human civilization and soil life. Yet, the net result of all the work and living done by soil inhabitants ends up looking much like the complex networks we rely on.

Some aspects of soil mimic Internet and telephone connections by creating communication and information networks between plants and soil life. Others are the factories and storage facilities where products are made, stored, or shipped from. Transportation networks exist to move residents and products like water and nutrients around. Plants, fungi, bacteria, and all the other organic and inorganic elements in soil interact in ways that resemble communities.

When you order heirloom seeds and they arrive in your mailbox, the order is the trigger and the seed arrival is the outcome. But all sorts of people and processes were involved in harvesting the seeds, packaging, transporting, and delivering processes. There were also the supporting players making envelopes, maintaining vehicles, moving fuel around, etc. Everyone was just living their lives as they chose to do. Yet, the established networks of communication, transportation, and protocols brought a level of automation to the whole transaction.

The same thing happens in healthy soil. A plant places an order for nutrients. Then, through millions of miniscule, non-automated transactions, the soil system delivers them. In damaged soil, those networks still exist, they just don't function so well. A plant may place an order for water or nitrogen and the order arrives late, in the wrong quantity, or not at all.

Conventional gardeners navigate broken soil systems by supplying plants with fast-acting fertilizer, irrigation, weed killer, and pesticides. That works to an extent because we know enough about plant biology to make reasonable guesses about how to manage their care. The problem is those plants are still plugged into the soil. So, the soil still gets all sorts of signals and orders from plants. That causes confusion and duplicate efforts that often lead to weeds coming to help with the cleanup. Broken networks with mixed signals are more weed-prone.

Organic gardeners try to give the soil system what it needs to get back into good working order. That way, once the automated networks are back online, plants can manage their own health. And, frankly, when tapped into healthy soil, plants do a much better job at it than we can. However, to get to that place of highly functional soil and plants that take care of themselves, we must improve the soil. For most soils, that involves these four steps.

1) Improve drainage.

2) Add organic matter.

3) Increase mycorrhizal networks.

4) Store more carbon.

I've put these in numbered order because that's the sequence that will help you transform your soil. However, it helps to think of these like a treadmill set on a steep incline at first. You'll need to cycle through them several times, in various ways, before soil health recovers. Then, as you make progress, the slope levels and the treadmill belt slows. Finally, one day the treadmill transforms into a cushy garden chaise lounge.

Step 1: Improve Drainage

To understand drainage, let's take a comprehensive look at how water moves through and gets stored in soil. Then, we can get into techniques for improving drainage in soil and issues in your landscape.

SOIL DRAINAGE

Water is the difference between life and no life in soil. Yet it's one of the least understood parts of gardening. We use rules of thumb like "plants need 1 inch (2.5 cm) of rain a week." I've repeated this idea myself in the past. But it's rarely true and this misconception leads to weeds.

The amount of water your plants need depends on the condition of your soil, the temperatures outside, and the kind of plants you grow. One inch (2.5 cm) of rain on a 90°F (32°C) day is less useful to plants than on a 60°F (16°C) day. One inch (2.5 cm) percolating through well-draining soil is different than going through deadpan clay. In sandy soil, 1 inch (2.5 cm) of rain can be gone in minutes.

Just like water in a pond or a lake, what's at the surface is also quickly impacted by air temperatures and sunlight. It evaporates on hot days and freezes on cold days. If your plants only root in that zone, then you may need to water more than once a day in hot weather to keep plants and soil life healthy.

That's why the aim in weed-free gardening is to develop deeper soils with better long-term water retention. When plants can root down where temperatures and water availability are more stable, they can live healthier, lower stress lives. For that to happen, though, soil needs excellent gravitational and capillary water.

GRAVITATIONAL WATER

The water that infiltrates quickly through the large pore spaces of your soil, such as between grains of sand or pebbles, is called gravitational water. That's because gravity drains it out of your soil quite quickly. Having good gravitational water flow is what's critical after an epic rainstorm or if you overwater. If you don't have it, your soil gets boggy and plant roots rot. Then, only weeds with low oxygen needs will thrive.

If a plant gets dehydrated, applying gravitational water to the root zone is a temporary fix. But gravitational water isn't the water you want your plant to rely on. Otherwise, you might need to water twice a day (or weed twice a day if you don't water enough).

CAPILLARY WATER

Capillary water is stored in soil matter and by life-forms that live in soil. Like water in a faucet, it's administered to plants on demand through capillary action.

An easy way to understand capillary water is to dip the corner of a paper towel in water. The dry paper towel sucks up the water against the force of gravity and holds it in the carbon fibers. This same thing happens in soil. As water flows down into the ground, soil particles, organic matter (mainly carbon), and life-forms wick up moisture. Then, they hang onto it so it doesn't drain out as gravitational water.

Now, if you squeeze that wet paper towel, some of the water will come out. The paper towel will still be wet. That's because some of that water was held in loose tension, like a film on top of the paper towel, and is quick to release. But some also got bound more tightly with the fibers and doesn't release so easily except through evaporation. This also happens with soil particles. They'll hold loose water that plants can uptake in the short-term, with some water held in tighter tension more long-term. When plants start to run hot while trying to stay cool, the soil particles will give up some water held in tighter tension as emergency water.

The goal with capillary water is to store as much of it as possible, as deep as possible in the soil without conditions becoming boggy and low in oxygen. To do that, soil needs to contain materials with good capillary retention.

The primary sources of capillary water in soil are clay, mycorrhizae, and stable carbon. The capillary action from clay can complicate getting water to plants, in ways we'll cover in a moment. But mycorrhizae and stable carbon are ideal capillary water retention vessels, which is why increasing their content in soil is the easiest way to improve drainage.

CLAY HEAVY SOILS

When clay gets shaped like a scoop and is kept soaked with water, it makes a perfect pond liner. Meanwhile, if moist organic matter sits on top of level clay soil, it becomes a bog. When heated or dried, clay becomes a nonpermeable kilned pottery plate that deflects water and resists separating.

None of those situations are ideal in garden beds. That's why, when trying to improve drainage in clay, you must break up compaction before and during the process of increasing organic matter. Otherwise, the clay in your soil can create all sorts of weed-promoting situations.

So, let's look at some simple tools, ordered from least to most disruptive to soil life, to address compaction.

TOOL BAR

Use your body weight to force the broad fork into the ground. Then, lean back to lift the soil, allowing air and water to better penetrate.

BROAD FORK

The broad fork fits its name. It looks like a giant fork that you push into the soil. Then, you lean the arms of the fork back toward you to lever the soil up gently. In some soil, you slice through and remove the fork. In heavier soil or grassy areas, you have to back it out after lifting.

After using, give your soil a good watering to get the water down deep where the fork tines barely reached. Resist the urge to stomp down the area. Instead, treat the broad-forked area like eggshells that you don't want to break until your plants grow in again.

SOIL AERATOR

A standard, manual aerator punches holes in soil using stakes. You usually roll them over your soil to aerate. Or you can even wear them on shoes and walk around to do it. Manual aerators generally only surface aerate. They are good for improving minor compaction issues or as a first step in really shallow topsoil.

Core or plug aerators pull cork-like plugs of soil to allow air room to move below ground. (Similar to what the cicadas do when they burrow out.) Inexpensive home-use core aerators will go down a couple of inches (approximately 5 cm). But for deeper compaction issues, you need heavy machinery that can core down 4 to 8 inches (4 to 20 cm). These are commonly used in lawns but can be used to kick-start gardens, too.

This manual aerator is good to use before watering to help water penetrate deeper.

If your soil is deadpan and a broad fork or soil aerator can't break the surface, you'll need to use other options. You may need to till down several inches (approximately 5 cm) first and work in aged compost to prevent soil from settling back into a solid slab.

MANUAL TILLER

A tiller is anything that breaks up the soil. Manual tillers can be as simple as hand tools with small rakes. Hoes and edgers can also do simple tilling in narrow rows, such as for planting seeds.

For larger areas, a simple standing twist tiller can break up compaction in the top few inches (approximately 7.5 cm) of soil and rip up shallow-rooted weeds at the same time. Just press the pronged bottom into the soil. Then turn the handlebars about a half circle. Lift out the prongs and repeat in the adjacent soil.

MACHINE TILLER

Machine tillers are usually gas powered and need to be pushed through soil. They are often heavy and not always easier on the back than twist tillers. The wheels and prongs below turn the soil up similar to the manual tiller, but at a much faster rate. Most machine tillers, especially home landscape models, tend to till down about 4 to 6 inches (10 to 15 cm). Commercial-rated tillers can go down below 6 inches (15 cm).

This simple twist tiller can turn up a patch of land in a few minutes to solve compaction problems in small areas.

This is the same clay shown in the turd test in Part 1 (see page 78). I just let it sit out at 80°F (27°C) for two days. It took some work to break it into these pieces to demonstrate the layers of compaction.

Besides addressing compaction, increasing the capillary action in clay also requires caution because clay is highly reactive with nutrients in organic matter. It can easily bind up nutrients. It also encourages bacterial life that can use up the miniscule amounts of air between small clay particles, making the soil susceptible to becoming anerobic. That leads to bogginess.

Conventional gardeners infuse air into clay soil with regular tilling. But that decreases water retention by drying the clay out. It also disrupts the soil networks we're working to repair. Rather than tilling, use plant roots to move organic matter and water deeper into clay soil. Tillage crops

like radish, mangels, and sweet potatoes (that die in winter in cold climates) can be used to create those organic matter and moisture mineshafts we covered in Part 1.

You can also use a broad fork periodically. When tillage crops and the broad fork aren't deep enough, then it's time to plant deep-rooted perennials, like trees or well-anchored shrubs. Alternatively, in an annual garden, you can rotate in deep-rooted, long-standing taprooted crops, like sesame for seeds or okra. With clay, you must find ways to continually break up compaction without disturbing soil networks to make lasting improvements to drainage.

WEED WHACK!

DOUBLE DIGGING

Another method used to break up compaction is double digging. This involves digging out the top 1 foot (30 cm) of soil over an area using a shovel. Then use a tiller to loosen the soil below. After that, mix the top 1 foot (30 cm) of soil with equal parts compost and put it back in place. At the end of the process, your bed looks raised because of the new compost. But it will quickly settle as soil life works that compost deeper down.

Rather than work a large area all at once, dig 2 feet (60 cm) at a time and use a wheelbarrow to mix up the soil. This process is a lot of work. It also triggers crazy weeds if you don't keep it heavily planted with fast-growing plants for several years afterwards. But for severely compacted clay, it may be the only way to break up compaction enough to improve water movement.

SAND-BASED SOILS

With sandy soils, increasing organic matter dramatically improves water retention. That can happen relatively quickly, too, since water helps organic matter percolate down into the soil profile. However, sandy soils don't support nearly the amount of soil life that clay can at the start. Without help from soil life, amendments don't get broken down into stable form.

For sandy soils, use soil improvement processes that increase bacterial activity. Incorporating a handful of vermicompost into every square foot (30 square cm) of soil can help. Use your fingertips to massage worm castings into the top 2 inches (5 cm) of the soil, then let water and plants do the rest. Regular use of organic liquid fertilizers also increases bacteria while feeding plants until the soil is ready to supply those nutrients.

Feeding partially composted materials to worms reduces wait time and makes it easier to produce a lot of vermicompost with minimal work shredding materials into smaller pieces.

WEED WHACK!

MAKE VERMI-COMPOST

Vermicompost is worm poop that gets further decomposed by soil bacteria without ever getting hot. Most people start the process by chopping up greens and browns to feed to worms in a small bin instead of putting it in their compost pile. However, you can make what I call vermi-compost if you instead feed your worms partially finished compost.

Make your compost pile however you normally do. Turn it once. Then, while you still have materials that haven't fully decomposed, spread the pile out to about 1 foot (30 cm) tall. Water any dry parts of the pile. Then make small divots throughout and tuck in some red wrigglers (bought online or from other gardeners).

Cover the pile with 2 inches (5 cm) of straw so the worms will work the surface

of the pile first. Keep that area moist with regular watering. A few weeks later, remove the straw to drive the worms deeper down. A couple of weeks after that, you can harvest vermi-compost to a depth of 1 to 2 inches (2.5 to 5 cm) at a time, starting at the top to drive worms deeper. Repeat until worms are condensed in the bottom of the pile, then scoop that last bit up and move the worms to a new location.

If you make a new compost pile right next to your first one, once that pile cools, start harvesting from the side furthest from the new pile. That will drive worms over into their new partially composted bed. Then, you can add being a *worm herder* to your garden resume.

The vermi-compost you remove needs to be aged for a couple of months before use. But this method makes so much more of it than tiny worm bins do that it will totally be worth the wait.

A standard organic garden recommendation is to apply mulch and compost so you can water less often. However, that recommendation is only true if the soil below is already well-draining. In poorly drained soils, adding compost and mulch won't reduce the need to water. Also, applying these non-strategically can trigger a continuous supply of problem-solving weeds. Here's how.

- Mulches that contain nitrogen, too thickly applied, can excite bacteria so much that they heat the soil and trigger evaporation.

- Mulches that compress in heavy rains, such as shredded wood mulches, can prevent water from passing through to the soil below.

- Mulches that are more permeable, like straw or pebbles, provide less water retention capacity. They also dry and warm quickly in hot weather, making the soil just below more volatile, temperature-wise.

- Sifted compost and finely chopped leaf mold are permeable while being better for moisture retention than faster draining mulches. But in organic matter-depleted soils, they get used up so quickly by soil life and plants that you may need to apply multiple times per year for moisture retention benefits.

Eventually, with regular applications of mulch and organic matter, your soil profile deepens, carbon gets stored, and mycorrhizal networks expand. Then, plants root deeper, stay cooler, use less water, and access capillary water with ease. Their healthy, abundant leaves also shade the soil, which keeps things cooler even at the surface. Until that happens, though, frequent, deep watering is mandatory to keep moving your soil quality in the healthy direction.

WEED WHACK!

BE A PALM READER

Want to know whether or not to water on a warm day? Become a palm reader.

Move aside your mulch and place your palm flat on your soil. If your soil doesn't feel noticeably cooler than the air temperatures above, C3 plants will start to draw up water from the soil below to stay cool. Water deeply right away to keep dehydrated soil from triggering soil-protecting heat-loving weeds.

LANDSCAPE DRAINAGE

Soil drainage is what you manage in your garden beds. But landscape drainage also needs to be managed for garden health and weed reduction. This includes all the water that runs over your paths, down your slopes, off hard surfaces, and potentially ends up as water in your garden beds. For example, in dry areas, if you get seasonal rains, then to improve drainage you may want to use channels called swales to redirect it in your garden. In wet areas, you may have to redirect water away for your beds or to use raised beds. In both dry and wet regions, you may want to collect rainwater in barrels or impoundments so you can use it on demand rather than have it fall in a rush on your beds.

This simple French drain catches water from one of our outbuildings and redirects the water away from the foundation of the building. But this idea can also be used in gardens.

The ideas that follow are meant to give you some ideas that might help with minor landscape drainage issues that can disturb your planting beds. However, before you use them, do additional research to confirm compatibility with your soil type and applicable legal codes.

FRENCH DRAIN

A French drain is an 8- to 24-inch-deep (20- to 61-cm) trench in the soil, backfilled with gravel, used to whisk water from a higher to a lower elevation using gravity. When used around building foundations or nonpermeable soil types, pipes with perforations on the top are laid in the trench to collect water and move it downhill to storm drains or more permeable soil. French drains can be used in the garden, such as to redirect water away from a retaining wall or to keep excess water from running directly into your planting area during heavy rains.

This gravel field is below grade on well-draining soil. It catches all the runoff that comes from an adjacent slope. If this fills up, it overflows to a low point outside of my garden.

This dry creek bed flows from the woods into a swale and rain garden.

INFILTRATION OR PERCOLATION TRENCH OR BASIN

A variation on a French drain, often called an infiltration or percolation trench or basin, is another alternative for improving drainage in the garden. These are shallow gravel trenches that function as short-term water impoundments to help water filter deeper into the soil profile rather than running off to a lower area.

The catchment area can be slightly sloped or more pond-like in shape. But like any dammed water area, these need a spillway to direct water overflow. You'll also want to do a percolation test, similar to those used for gray water systems or septic tanks, to make sure your soil is permeable enough to allow the water to infiltrate deeply. Otherwise, these might become ponds in rainy periods.

DRY CREEK BEDS

Dry creek beds are another variation on French drains or drainage basins. They can be made by manipulating the contours of your landscape or dug in and backfilled with materials to give them more aesthetic appeal. Dry creek beds work best when they are mildly sloped so they don't run like rivers. They also need to be compacted so they don't turn into bogs. Finally, they eventually need to outlet to a safe location, such as to a rain garden.

Rain gardens are a great way to capture and collect rainwater. They drain quickly and are planted with species that tolerate intermittent floods.

RAIN GARDENS

Rain gardens are also a terrific drainage solution to collect and use water redirected by a French drain or a dry creek bed or as an alternative to an infiltration or percolation basin. They are often used along crowned driveways, to collect roof runoff, or at the bottom of short, shallow slopes.

These are pond-like depressions in the earth that collect runoff water and filter it deeper underground via the roots of plants. However, they are made using materials that drain quickly, like raised bed mix and wood chips. They are also filled with plants that have a high tolerance for short-term flooding and intermittent droughts. Rain gardens also need a low point so excess water can drain out and not turn beds into bogs.

My rain garden starts with a frog pond that overflows into a series of rain depressions running along the outside of my vegetable garden. This keeps the water from further uphill from overrunning my planting beds.

The large curly dock-covered mound in this photo is a hügelkultur. Adjacent is a swale path that I'm filling with gravel for better drainage. The seating area also doubles as an infiltration basin. Sometimes multiple solutions are necessary to manage water flow sufficiently.

SWALES

Swales are like scoops in the landscape that catch and move rain and runoff. In wet areas, they can redirect rain away from planted areas to prevent bogginess. In dry landscapes, they collect water and redirect it deeper into the soil just downslope of the swale to irrigate deep-rooted plants.

Swales require careful calculations and planning to work well. But they can do wonders to promote appropriate drainage in your garden. They can also dramatically reduce the necessity of watering in dry areas and help alter a slope to make it possible to plant.

MOUNDS

Mounds are upside-down swales. They can be used as planting zones in wet areas to drive water into the root zone and away from the top of the bed to prevent erosion and bogginess. They can be used like speed bumps to slow down water on a slope. They can also be used like the crown of a blacktop or concrete road to direct water off the mound area and down into swales or beds that collect it or move it.

HÜGELKULTUR

A hügelkultur is a special kind of mound that starts with some stacked decomposing tree trunks. On top of that base go stacks of smaller branches. Then even smaller stems and vegetative matter get piled over that. Finally, the whole area is covered with at least 6 inches (15 cm) or more of topsoil and a heavy mulch like double-shredded hardwood to hold the soil in place.

The finished bed ends up somewhere between 4 and 6 feet (1.2 and 1.8 m) tall and dome-shaped. To stabilize all that soil, immediately transplant in perennial seedlings and small fruits plus annuals like chard, kale, arugula, and other low-growing, aboveground harvested vegetables. As the materials in the mound decompose (starting with the small materials on the top, ending with the large materials on the bottom), they continuously feed soil life and plants.

In the right conditions, these beds act like sponges, sucking up extra water through the woody materials in the base and the planting and soil areas on top. Be careful, though. If the soil on top of the hügelkultur gets compacted, then this becomes a mound that just moves water down its sides into other areas that might not need it.

Step 2: Add Organic Matter

Besides understanding drainage, adding organic matter strategically is necessary to keep improving drainage deeper down in the soil profile. Organic matter is any recently deceased matter that's in various phases of decomposition. It includes things like mulch, dead insects, dead plant roots, insect frass (manure), bird droppings, and more. Compost and everything you put in it is also organic matter, but it's just a bit more decomposed than the other stuff.

Organic matter in all forms can be good for your garden. You just need to consider it's likely impacts to figure out when and how much can be safely applied. Let's look at the various types of organic matter you might want to use for your garden.

COMPOST

Composting converts raw carbon materials, nitrogen, and other nutrients into stable carbon that is chemically bonded with those nutrients. Similar to the paper towel example I gave earlier, the stable carbon made by composting wicks up nutrients and holds them longer and in tighter tension than raw carbon. Also, by applying compost rather than raw organic matter, we reduce the workload for soil life so they can focus on getting nutrients to plants.

These three different kinds of compost—leaf (top), cow manure-based (middle), and mushroom (bottom)—have a different impact on the soil. Leaf and mushroom are better for weed-prevention. Cow manure has more immediately available nutrients.

Save your browns and greens until you have enough to make a large enough pile to trigger thermophilic composting. After composting, age your materials before adding to your garden.

WEED WHACK!

MAKE THERMOPHILIC (HOT) COMPOST

At home, making thermophilic compost piles is one of the most controllable ways to create nutrient-rich stable carbon that will benefit your garden. You just need to stick to some basic guidelines.

- Target using materials that result in 24 to 40 parts carbon to 1 part nitrogen in the pile. (You can find a link to a carbon to nitrogen compost on my website at Simplestead.com/potager).

- Layer green (nitrogen-rich) materials with brown (carbon-rich) materials to promote good internal airflow for thermophilic (heat-loving) bacteria.

- Build the pile about 4 feet (1.2 m) tall and wide to ensure sufficient thermal mass for rapid decomposition.

- Water materials to about 60 percent of their saturation potential during composting.

- Give the pile a few days to heat up and cool down. Once it starts generating heat, use a compost thermometer to make sure it gets to about 135°F (57°C). (If it doesn't, try watering with manure-laced water or turning the pile and adding in some fresh layers.) Then, wait for the pile to cool enough to turn.

- Turn the pile so external materials become internal materials. Monitor the temperature again and after it heats up and then cools down, turn it again. Repeat the turning process until most of the materials are decomposed past recognition.

- Age the pile for at least six months, but preferably longer, to allow the thermophilic bacteria to go dormant and cooler temperature soil-benefiting bacteria to colonize the pile.

Thermophilic composting triggers weed seeds into early germination and their germplasm are killed by heat. It also damages seeds that don't germinate, making the weeds that grow from them weaker and easier to control. Aging before applying encourages beneficial bacteria and reduces weed risks from excess nutrients.

The slow pile method, where you just layer materials as you go and then let it stand for a couple of years until it's finally compost, also works great. But it's weedier in the long run. If you do use the slow pile method, you may still need to turn the pile to prevent rot spots. Keep it covered with straw to reduce weed seed germination and pick out weeds as they start. And age it for at least a year after it looks like compost to reduce the risk of pathogens.

These are some of the mulch trial beds I've been experimenting with. There are all kinds of mulches with varying risks and benefits that need to be weighed before you apply.

MULCHES

Besides compost, other forms of organic matter that we use on or around beds to support soil life are collectively referred to as "mulches." Mulch always goes on top of soil. It can be just about anything. However, for deciding how to use them in the garden, consider their impact on soil.

High-carbon materials, such as wood-based mulches, are slow to decompose and less likely to hot compost in small quantities. When these come into contact with sufficient water and nitrogen, though, they can still hot compost.

High-nitrogen materials are mainly fresh vegetative matter, like grass clippings and greens. They contain their own nitrogen and water, which makes them attractive to bacterial decomposers and prone to rotting. However, they only turn hot when mixed with additional carbon.

Let's take a closer look at both types.

HIGH-CARBON MULCHES

High-carbon mulches aren't the same kind of stable, processed carbon that results after you make compost. If you were to make a 4 x 4-foot (1.2 x 1.2-m) pile and pour nitrogen-rich rainwater through these mulches, they'd heat up in no time. If you bury high-carbon mulches, microlife will collect all the nitrogen in the soil and create an underground compost pile to decompose these in a hurry.

That's why it's important to only use high-carbon mulches in small amounts to avoid hot composting in contact with soil so they don't temporarily rob your plants of water and nutrient access. Since high-carbon mulches borrow resources—namely nitrogen—from soil, don't consider them a nutrient source when first applied. It can take a few months for them to start supplying the soil with nutrients when top applied.

Wood-based Mulches

Wood-based mulches include chips, bark nuggets, and shreds made primarily of the non-leafy portion of trees and shrubs. Softwoods like pine or poplar decompose faster than hardwoods like oak or maple. Rot-resistant woods like black locust, cedar, and redwood are slow to decompose. However, they may have fungal suppressing properties that also slow down some beneficial soil fungi processes.

All wood-based mulches are subject to termite infestations. That makes them risky to use directly around any woody infrastructure (like your timber-framed house).

Processed woods like paper, cardboard, sawdust, and kiln-dried pine shavings are also wood-based mulches. However, that processing makes them decompose faster in contact with soil. They need to be used sparingly as a mulch. Or, better yet, use them mainly in the compost pile.

Brown Leaf and Needle Mulches

Brown leaf or needle mulches are made from leaves or needles that fall to the ground when they are already mostly depleted of nutrients. These are nature's favorite mulch. You can safely use them, like nature does, by spreading a couple of inches (approximately 5 cm) under plants in fall and letting them decompose in place.

When you chop or grind them into smaller sizes, they are prone to fast decomposition. That makes them a risk when applied too thickly on beds. If you want to use mulched leaves or needles, make them into leaf mold before applying. This will reduce their weed-triggering potential and also expedite their benefits to the soil life below.

Soil loves carbon and most soils are so short on it that it's ideal to use high-carbon mulches, in small quantities, as fast as your soil can process them. Just be careful to avoid some of the potential downsides with these application tips.

WEED WHACK!

MAKE LEAF MOLD

Leaf mold is partially decomposed leaf matter that is high in stable carbon, but still low in nitrogen. It's my favorite free semi-stable carbon source to use with clay soils.

Mulch the leaves that come down in fall with a leaf mulcher or by running over them with a bag lawn mower to chop and suck them up. Put the chopped leaves in black plastic bags with the top open. Or pile them up in a compost bin. When the leaf mass shrinks to about a quarter of the original size and turns from brown in color to closer to black, use them like aged compost under your plants.

Note: Lots of people spray trees with materials that would be toxic to young plants. Bioassay free leaves or leaf mold from neighbors or municipal sources before use.

- Don't mix these into soil or you'll bind up nutrients and use up water.
- Don't add more than a couple of inches (approximately 5 cm) at a time around or on garden beds, or they'll be prone to hot composing or bogginess when wet.
- Avoid direct contact with plant stems to keep them from rotting.
- Apply in cool weather so the high-carbon matter in contact with soil will get processed into more stable carbon before warmer weather might increase risk for hot composting.

- Move the mulch before you apply liquid fertilizer to the soil to avoid triggering rapid decomposition.
- Don't let these mulches compact, or they'll reduce water and airflow into soil.
- Be ready to rake mulches back out if they start warming up, bogging down, or otherwise having a negative impact on your other plants.

High-Carbon Mulches for Weed Control and Soil Improvement

MULCH NAME	CARBON TO NITROGEN RATIO
Cardboard	350:1
Coconut Husks and Shells	180:1
Hardwood Bark	220:1
Hardwood Mulch/Chips	560:1
Leaves (Dried)	60:1
Newspaper	450:1
Pine Needles	80:1
Sawdust	325:1
Softwood Bark	500:1
Softwood Mulch/Chips	640:1
Straw (Barley)	85:1
Straw (Oat)	60:1
Straw (Wheat)	120:1
Wood Chips (Mixed)	400:1

Apply these in cool weather and in small amounts to prevent hot composting.

HIGH-NITROGEN MULCHES

On the other side of the mulch spectrum are the high-nitrogen mulch sources. These are things like fresh grass clippings, mowed-down cover crops, or green manures like comfrey.

If applied when freshly cut, they come with a lot of water content stored in the leaves and stems. They also have nitrogen built into their leaves. So, unlike with high-carbon mulches, high-nitrogen mulches don't normally rob your soil of moisture or nutrients when applied. Though, for hay, since it's dry, you'll want to water it when you apply.

High-nitrogen mulches come with other risks, though. First, during decomposition they can release strong nutrients that invite weeds and harm low-fertility loving plants. Second, thick applications may raise soil temperatures during decomposition. Third, if you collect these from other people's gardens, they may contain fresh herbicide residues that will lead to more weeds down the road. Finally, they temporarily occupy the same soil life that would otherwise help your plants.

Generally, when using high-nitrogen mulches, applying a few weeks before planting is ideal. Also use a light-blocking cover, such as landscape fabric, to reduce weed germination until you can plant.

Quick to decompose, these are best applied regularly in small amounts for weed prevention and feeding soil life.

High-Nitrogen Mulches for Weed Control and Soil Improvement

MULCH NAME	CARBON TO NITROGEN RATIO
Ashes, Wood	25:1
Grass Clippings	20:1
Green Manure	20–30:1*
Hay (Grass)	40:1
Hay (Legume)	20:1
Leaves (Fresh)	35:1
Leaves (Green, Dried)	45:1
Shrub Trimmings	50:1
Tree Trimmings	20:1
Weeds (Dried)	20:1
Weeds (Fresh)	10:1

*C:N varies based on maturity at time of cutting and fibrousness of materials.

WEED WHACK!

GROW YOUR OWN HIGH-NITROGEN MULCHES

Green manures and cover crops are two tools you can use to make your own high-nitrogen mulch.

COVER CROPS

I mentioned cover crops in Part 1 for use in working soil amendments into soil (see page 31). But they can also be used whenever necessary to address imbalances in the soil or as soil protection between planting other crops. They are also a good way to get more carbon in your soil by using the sun. I highly recommend growing them anytime you have gaps in your planting calendar in an annual garden. It's less work than weeding and prettier, too.

This buckwheat is just about ready to mow down.

20 Cover Crops for Soil Improvement and Weed Suppression

NAME	CARBON: NITROGEN	BENEFITS
Annual rye	26:1	Spring or summer coverage, nutrient gleaning, allelopathic
Austrian peas	17:1	Nitrogen fixing, carbon increasing
Barley	20:1	Spring or summer coverage, nutrient laundering, allelopathic
Buckwheat	34:1	Fast-growing, soil covering, carbon increasing, nutrient laundering
Cowpeas	21:1	Nitrogen fixing, carbon increasing
Fava beans	17:1	Nitrogen fixing, carbon increasing
Fenugreek	17:1	Nitrogen fixing, carbon increasing
Field turnips	Root 14:1, Shoots 12:1	Fast-growing, carbon increasing, nutrient laundering, soil tilling
Hairy vetch	11:1	Nitrogen fixing, carbon increasing
Mangel	Root 40:1, Shoots 11:1	Normally grown as fodder, but good for soil tilling too
Millet (German foxtail)	44:1	Fast-growing, soil covering, carbon increasing, nutrient laundering
Millet (Japanese)	42:1	Fast-growing, soil covering, carbon increasing, nutrient laundering
Millet (Pearl)	50:1	Fast-growing, soil covering, carbon increasing, nutrient laundering
Mustard	26:1	Allelopathic, fast-growing, soil covering, carbon increasing, nutrient laundering, fungal pathogen suppressing
Oats	12:1	Fast-growing, soil covering, carbon increasing, nutrient laundering
Perennial rye	26:1	Long-term cover, soil-depth increasing, nutrient laundering, allelopathic
Sorghum-sudangrass	20:1	Fast-growing, soil covering, carbon increasing, nutrient laundering, soil tilling
Sweet potatoes	20:1	Fast-growing, carbon increasing, nutrient laundering, soil tilling, vining-shade cover
Tillage radish	Root 32:1, Shoots 16:1	Fast-growing, carbon increasing, nutrient laundering, soil tilling
Winter wheat	14:1	Fall to spring coverage, nutrient laundering, allelopathic

For carbon to nitrogen ratios of 24:1 or less, you only need to wait a couple of weeks to plant. For ratios of 25:1 or more, wait until the materials are mostly decomposed to start new plants direct in the soil.

LIFE-CYCLE	SEASON	METHOD TO KILL AND NOTES ON USE
Annual	Cool	Spring planted: Repeat mowing at flowering, plant 40-50 days before frost for frost kill
Annual	Cool	Winter killed at 5°F (-15°C), otherwise prevent flowering, repeat mow and mulch; use with inoculant for nitrogen fixation
Annual	Cool	Repeat mowing at flowering, plus paper/mulch cover; cold tolerance varies by cultivar
Annual	Warm	Repeat mowing at flowering
Annual	Warm	Repeat mowing at flowering; use with inoculant for nitrogen fixation
Annual	Cool	Repeat mowing at flowering; use with inoculant for nitrogen fixation
Annual	Cool	Repeat mowing at flowering; use with inoculant for nitrogen fixation
Annual	Cool	Winter killed at 20°F (-7°C), otherwise repeat mow
Perennial	Cool	Use for several years, then suppress by light deprivation; use with inoculant for nitrogen fixation
Annual	Cool	Repeat mowing at flowering
Non-hardy perennial	Warm	Prevent flowering, frost killed
Non-hardy perennial	Warm	Prevent flowering, frost killed
Non-hardy perennial	Warm	Prevent flowering, frost killed
Annual	Cool	Repeat mowing at flowering
Annual	Cool	Prevent flowering, winter killed at 5°F (-15°C)
Perennial	Cool	Use for several years, then suppress by light deprivation
Annual	Warm	Repeat mow to ground when plants are 3 feet (1 m) high
Annual in cold climates	Warm	Frost killed, not advised as cover crop in warm climates since it can be a hard-to-kill perennial
Annual	Cool	Winter killed at 20°F (-7°C), otherwise repeat mow
Annual	Cool	Repeat mowing at flowering

Sterile comfrey is my favorite green manure. You can mow it down four or five times a year and it will keep on making more leaf mass.

WEED WHACK!

GREEN MANURE

When you grow plants to harvest and use on another bed, these are called green manure. Unlike animal manure, green manure is safe to apply when fresh without the pathogen risks that come from manure.

Many organic gardeners grow deep-rooted perennial plants as green manure. Comfrey and stinging nettle (harvested with gloves) are the two most commonly grown plants as compost additives. But any plant that grows well in your area and makes a lot of fast-decomposing leaf mass can be green manure.

I grow mints for this purpose, too. Lemon balm, apple mint, and anise hyssop are my favorite green manure mints because they don't regrow as easily from cut stems as peppermint or spearmint do. I also grow weedy plants like curly dock and large-leaved amaranths as green manure.

Use green manures the same as you would other high-nitrogen mulches. But take note: Because you are taking minerals from one part of your garden to another, you create a net nutrient and carbon gain where applied. Of course, you also get a net nutrient loss but possible carbon gain from where you harvest.

Sometimes, you may need to pull excess minerals out of beds if you overapply the same kind of compost or mulches. For example, heavy use of manure-based compost can result in excess phosphorous in the soil. Cover crops like crimson clover and tillage radish or field turnips draw these up in their leaves. So, if you mow and harvest the tops a few times to use in other beds, you can draw out some excess phosphorous. Then, you can still leave the roots in place to benefit the soil where they grew. Excess nitrogen can be drawn up by grasses like millet, wheat, or barley that are mowed and moved to other beds rather than allowed to form seed heads.

Those weed niche identification skills we covered in Part 1 can help you identify mineral imbalances. Then you can use your analogous plant selection skills to grow the right kind of green manure to solve the issue. Of course, you can also just let the weeds do the work, then mow their leaves to use as green manure. Just be careful not to let them seed.

PICKING THE RIGHT ORGANIC MATTER TO USE AS MULCH

We've covered a lot of details on mulches. The real weed-free gardening skill to master, though, is picking the right mulch to fit your budget and the condition of your soil.

New beds will have a lot of weeds. Also, the soil networks aren't well established and so pretty much anything you do will be an improvement. In those areas, I add as much organic matter in any form as I can.

For example, I might make compost piles right on those beds in fall. Then in spring, I'll rake out that fresh compost to just a few inches (approximately 7.5 cm) high. I'll cover the fresh compost with some of my long-aged compost to plant cover crops in. I'll put straw around the cover crops to keep weeds down until they cover the area. Then I'll mow the cover crops down as mulch. A few weeks later I'll plant some deep-rooting cover crops to move materials on top down deeper. I'll mow their tops a few times until they die. Then I'll start a fall cover crop.

The following spring, the bed is usually ready for more cultivated plants. At that point, for perennial plants, I'll start to use high-carbon mulches. Perhaps I'll use leaf mold the first year and then alternate between wood-based mulch and leaf mulch as needed after that.

For vegetable beds, after the cover crops I transition to aged compost—made with as many different materials as possible— added on top of soil before replanting. I'll also mix in vermicompost whenever I can. Plus, after planting, I'll rotate in light layers of straw, cover crops, and green manure to keep it lively.

All mulches reduce weeds by minimizing soil disturbance and reducing seed germination due to light exposure. But make sure you cycle in those deep-rooted plants to move nutrients further down to increase soil depth faster.

HUMIC CONTENT

There's one last soil detail that we need to cover, one that relates to the addition of organic matter. Humus, humic acid, fulvic acid, and humin are all components of what's referred to as humic content in soil. Humic content is one of those mysteries that we simply don't understand well.

What we know is that the more you have, the better the health of your plants and all the life in your soil. Even with as little as 2 percent humic content, soil will retain more water longer.

You can't technically add pure humus directly to your soil because it's inseparable from soil except by chemical extraction. You can buy a mined substance called lignite (a kind of coal), sold in granular form, that will convert to humic and fulvic acids in contact with soil and water. You can also buy liquid humic and fulvic acids that have been chemically separated from soil or compost containing humic content for quick application.

None of these products is the same composition as the humic content in healthy soil. But they may temporarily influence water availability and nutrient uptake around plant roots when applied to a planting hole or during watering. They're expensive, and we don't really know how effective they are relative to just adding compost or mulch. If you choose to use them, consider them a supplement to your normal additions of organic matter, not a substitute.

Compost will contain some humic content and make more when it integrates into soil. The mulches you add will also be the feedstock your soil uses to make more of it. Even though we are pretty in the dark on why humic content is so key to healthy soils, we are certain that it is. Research also suggests that humic content and mycorrhizal networks are probably linked and may increase together.

Step 3: Increase Mycorrhizal Networks

Mycorrhizae are soilborne fungi that help provide plants with nutrients and moisture in exchange for plant sugars via plant root systems. There are two primary kinds—arbuscular and ectomycorrhizal.

Arbuscular mycorrhizae penetrate the root systems of plants they serve and directly disperse nutrients or water. These thrive around plants that have more regular nutrient demands such as around most of the plants we grow in our gardens.

Ectomycorrhizal fungi collaborate with plants that thrive in slower nutrient soil environments like established forests. They make nutrients and moisture available around the deeper root zones, but they don't penetrate the root system.

Both of these groups of fungi create complex networks of hyphae, or threadlike structures, that are collectively called mycelium. When soil is not regularly disturbed, this mycelium can expand its populations and occupy much of the space between particles of soil. Then, when gravitational water falls through soil particles, it soaks it up like sponges. Small networks may not be visible. Larger networks can end up looking like mushroom blocks that oyster mushrooms are grown on.

In essence, mycelium create a water tank for plants. These tiny sponges also suck up nutrients and hang on to them so they don't wash away. Then they make nutrients available to plants on demand. They also play a central role in stabilizing carbon in the soil and likely increasing humic content.

Fungi experts say that over 90 percent of plants form relationships with mycorrhizae. So, rather than tell you all the plants that need more mycorrhizae in soil, let me tell you about the handful that don't directly collaborate with them. Brassicaceae (e.g., cabbage, mustard), Amaranthaceae (e.g. spinach, chard), Caryophyllaceae (e.g., dianthus), and the low-pH-loving members of the Vaccinium (e.g., blueberry, cranberry) and Ericaceae (e.g. rhododendron, azalea) families aren't mycorrhizally-affiliated.

Everything else in your garden will benefit directly from increasing the mycorrhizal networks and populations in your soil. Even those non-mycorrhizal plants may benefit from the improvements like increased humic content that come from having thriving mycorrhizal networks.

My experiments have convinced me beyond a shadow of a doubt that encouraging them reduces weeds by making my plants happier and healthier. They also occupy the soil space where plants can't. Plus, they stabilize nutrients for long-term storage. That means fewer weeds come to solve open soil and nutrient depletion and excess issues. Mycorrhizae are an incredible soil stabilizer that makes weed outbreaks from stressed-out plant and soil life signals less likely to occur.

Improving drainage and adding organic matter are two actions that help increase mycorrhizal communities. The next step, though, is to stock your soil with perennial plants that collaborate with mycorrhizae.

Any perennial plants that are direct mycorrhizal beneficiaries can be hosts for increasing mycorrhiza in soil. I've had my best success using dry-loving aromatic perennial herbs like rosemary, lavender, sage, clary sage, and wormwood. Other leafy herbs like comfrey, lambs' ears, and evening primrose also noticeably increase colonization levels. Trees and shrubs do as well, but the smaller shrubs and leafy vegetative herbs seem to work best.

I grow these perennial herbs throughout my garden beds between my annuals to act as long-term hosts for mycorrhizae. I also grow my vegetable beds between longer aisles of perennial edibles like apples, mints, blackberry, asparagus, wild arugula, and other perennials. Essentially, the more mycorrhizal-loving perennials you can fit in between your annuals the better the soil and plant health for annuals.

Also, rotate your annuals so those non-arbuscular mycorrhizal (AM) affiliated plants like cabbage, broccoli, mustard, spinach, kale, and other brassica and amaranth family plants don't dominate the beds. Alternatively, interplant those non-AM veggies with annual herbs that grow for most of the season.

Additionally, using high-quality arbuscular mycorrhizal inoculants from reputable sellers can fast-track the colonization. These are applied like fertilizer in the planting hole or dissolved in water and poured through soil. Choose inoculants that have multiple species of mycorrhizae known to be beneficial to the kind of plants you mostly grow. Product sellers should be able to refer you to scientific research that applies to your plants. Or, they may have the information already available on their blogs. Note: You don't have to buy these; mycorrhizae will come (probably in bird poop). But they do speed things up in a new garden.

These first three steps to getting soil in top condition for weed-free gardening—improving drainage, adding organic matter, and increasing mycorrhizal connections—are all deeply interrelated, as you can see. They are also the groundwork for step 4—store more carbon—the most important improvement you can do for your garden, and our planet, that we'll cover in Part 3.

THE WORLD OF WEEDS

When I lived on Maui for a year, it seemed like heaven on earth. You could visit ten different ecosystems ranging from tropical rain forests to uninhabitable dry desert in a single day without even getting out of your car. Every fourth species of marine life in the reefs around the island evolved there in isolation over tens of thousands of years, making it a sanctuary of diversity. Yet, when thousands of humpback whales the size of buses funneled into the channel in winter to breed and give birth in a ritual migration that started in Alaska and spanned half the globe, it made me realize that Maui is just a tiny part of a much larger paradise.

Planet Earth, like Maui, is an island so isolated that it has evolved countless endemic species, not likely to be found anywhere else in the universe. This incredible world we live in really is heaven on earth. If you spend just a few minutes each day considering the complexity of life at work even in the growing of one single weed, it's hard not to be completely awed and humbled by sheer wonder.

The visible and invisible network of life beneath the soil is critical for plant health.

Just to give you a sense of how much diversity of life we're talking about, one study revealed that the little bit of soil that stuck to a single beet contained 33,000 different species of bacteria and over 10 billion individual bacteria. There are also roughly 57 billion nematodes for every person on Earth spread over 80,000 species, and most of them live in soil. There are 70,000 identified species of fungi and likely as many as 1.5 million not yet identified that all contribute in some fashion to the soil composition that influences plant growth. It's been estimated that if you took the top 6 to 7 inches (15-18 cm) of soil on an acre of land and sifted out just the microlife, it could add up to several tons in weight.

Life is interacting—constantly. The amount of data transferred in soil is magnitudes of order greater than the tiny fraction of 24,000 gigatons humans move across the Internet each second.

Similar to the way we pass information and goods over the Internet and with vehicles, soil life sends goods, like nutrients, and information, like pest alerts, across networks of connectivity collectively referred to as the rhizosphere. That rhizosphere exists even in the soil that accumulates in the crack in a sidewalk.

Given all that interaction, though, what's equally unnerving is that some species of plants are able to cause massive rhizosphere upheaval—on an apocalyptic scale from the perspective of soil life—simply by growing in a new location. These plants possess what's called allelopathy. It's the ability to exude chemicals into the soil, either by roots or during decomposition, and radically alter the behavior of other-life forms.

Garlic mustard (*Alliaria petiolate*) is one of these allelopathic plants that has forest managers in North America on high alert. In some locations, the plant has been found to exude metabolites from its roots that can cause a decline in ectomycorrhizal fungi. In other places, garlic mustard may cultivate relationships with pathotrophic, or potentially harmful, fungi that can be detrimental to neighboring plants' health. It may also encourage bacterial development that slows carbon cycling capacity for other plants, stunting their growth and giving garlic mustard a size advantage.

The exact nature of garlic mustard's allopathy and the extent of its destruction on forest ecology is something researchers are still working to understand.

Interestingly, though, there are also some studies that suggest garlic mustard may cultivate bacteria that increase quantities of plant-available nitrogen and phosphorous. If trees then used those freed-up nutrients to grow bigger, faster, they might offset carbon sequestration losses in the soil with carbon increases in their trunks and branches.

Unfortunately, garlic mustard is also displacing lots of native plants in its path.

In its native range, garlic mustard isn't terribly invasive. It's controlled by insect pests that devour its leaves and humans who harvest it for pesto. While it likely alters soil life in Europe too, hungry pests and chefs make those impacts more negligible. Some research also suggests that after a few decades of destructive soil activity, garlic mustard populations naturalize, and soil life rebounds for reasons we don't yet understand.

On a personal note, I can't help but see parallels between garlic mustard's impact on ecosystems and what we humans are doing. The way we displace native species and upset ecosystems sure looks like a net negative from a natural perspective. The rapid rate at which we are releasing climate-destabilizing carbon dioxide into the atmosphere is such an enormous threat to the stability of the planet that worrying about garlic mustard invasions almost seems insignificant. But what if, like garlic mustard in its native range, we could find ways to behave a lot less like an invasive species?

Personally, I believe we can. In our gardens, where we get to collaborate with nature to create our own visions of heaven on earth, we can help preserve natural diversity by growing as many plant species as possible and actively controlling invasive plants. We can also feed our soil with a wide variety of compost types and organic mulches to encourage complex systems of microlife.

By developing our deep and abiding love for nature and biodiversity, and gardening more like nature does, we can create microcosms of heaven on earth.

Garlic mustard is an example of an allelopathic plant.

PART THREE

RECONCILIATION

As I mentioned in the introduction, the word *weed* only gained importance post-WWII in conjunction with the increase in sales of herbicides. During that same time frame, another former chemical weapon also came into fashion as an agricultural resource: synthetic nitrogen fertilizer. By the late 1960s, synthetic fertilizer was standard in farming. All the former organic amendments that returned carbon and natural fertility to the soil fell by the wayside.

Soon after, synthetic fertilizer became a mainstay for home landscapes, too. Home gardeners stopped feeding their soil organic matter and instead started feeding plants directly. In just a few generations, gardeners transitioned from being soil fertility managers to fertilizer fretters. Since that shift, landscape soils have been rapidly losing their carbon stores to the atmosphere or erosion. All that excess carbon, in the form of carbon dioxide, is a big part of what's raising global average temperatures.

For the past 11,000 years since we started farming in earnest, we've released more carbon from the soil than we've put back. Yet, the most consequential losses of soil carbon have happened since those Green Revolution-popularized herbicides and synthetic fertilizers. Of course, much of the excess carbon also comes from fossil fuel use in agriculture and our daily lives.

"Plants can return carbon and natural fertility to the soil."

Not all of it can go back in our soil in the near-term. But as organic gardeners, we can take carbon from the air and put it into soil quickly. We've already talked about three big ways to improve soil health: improve drainage, add organic matter, and encourage mycorrhizae. Those three things—especially the use of organic matter, most of which is carbon—will go a long way toward turning our soils into carbon sinks again. But there's one more strategic way to move forward on healing soil and improving our shared environment.

Natural beds decompose into organic matter and large-leaved plants help store more carbon in the soil.

Before I say the magic word, though, let me tell you a funny, but also troubling, story about the state of our gardening knowledge today. One of the most common requests I get from gardeners is to look at their plants and tell them if I think they need more nitrogen. In response, I take a deep breath—78 percent of which is nitrogen. Then, I meditate for a moment on the 100-foot-tall (30-m) trees, shrubs, vines, and ground cover plants all around my forested region that live on nature-delivered nitrogen. Finally, I lean down and claw my fingers into the bone-dry, orange clay stuff their plants are dying in and reveal the real issue.

The darker soil on the left started out like the soil on the right only six months earlier. A ½-inch (1-cm) application of compost helped kick-start the shallow-rooted, fibrous weeds to store carbon and attract beneficial insects like worms to the surface of the soil.

Your soil needs more carbon, I tell them. That always leads to confused looks because they haven't seen carbon for sale at the store. Compost, yes, but carbon, no. Where do they go to get carbon? Is it expensive?

Twenty years ago, that could have been me wondering where to buy carbon. Today, though, the fact that so many people worry about nitrogen rather than soil health also makes me a little worried for our future.

Carbon and nitrogen are literally all around us; nature has already come up with incredible tools to help us get them into our soil. There are almost 400,000 different species of plants and more microlife than we'll ever count designed by nature to remove carbon from the air and put it in soil. Plus, an impressive decomposition system returns carbon- and nutrient-rich once-living organic matter to the soil. That same decomposition system also captures and converts the airborne and organic matter–based nitrogen into plant-usable nutrients.

If we can see the forest for the trees (or the garden for the weeds), the answers are there. Now, are you ready for that magic one-word solution to get more carbon back into your soil?

It's plants! When you improve drainage, add organic matter, and increase mycorrhizae, the last piece of the puzzle to store more carbon in soil is to grow as many plants as possible. That way, they move airborne carbon into the soil through photosynthesis.

I've given you some ideas on ways to increase your carbon-fixing plant count—like growing cover crops, mixing perennials with annuals, and rotating non-mycorrhizal plants or interplanting with them. We've also looked at some green manures and picking analogous plants to replace weeds based on things like root type, carbon fixation, and the conditions they prefer. But let me throw one more wild idea at you.

WHY NOT USE WEEDS?

Plants that fall into the weedy category are one of nature's best resources for sinking carbon back into the earth. Think of all those C4 carbon fixers in your garden in summer. Or of those adaptive behaviors that allow heat-loving plants to start early to establish deep roots before warm weather sets in. Research suggests that weeds are already increasing in number. They're expected to be more prolific in the future as a result of all the extra carbon in the air.

What niche do you think nature is filling by making weeds grow even more aggressively in a world where atmospheric carbon is rapidly increasing? Can you prevent those carbon-fixing weeds from getting into your garden given how little control you have over atmospheric carbon? And can you get enough carbon into your soil to fill that niche using only cultivated plants and additions of organic matter? Or, is it perhaps time to take some free help from nature to increase carbon in soil?

MARCH 2014

JUNE 2015

Weed-Free Carbon Gardening

Based on my own observations of weeds, I'm convinced they are growing bigger, faster, and more prolifically to help solve the carbon crisis. My experience in using them to do massive soil regeneration on a degraded mountainside over the last seven years has also persuaded me of their power to help sink carbon and make cultivated gardening so much easier.

If you want to start putting weedy plants to work increasing the carbon in your soil, I know a few ideas that can help. These suggestions are based on the core tenets of carbon-farming. However, I've adapted them based on my experience for use in the home landscape.

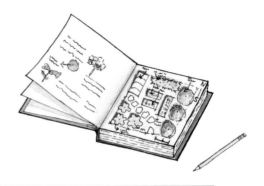

JULY 2021

When we moved to our homestead, we had no topsoil and barely any weeds grew. We added organic matter and addressed drainage and compaction issues. Weeds started showing up. We used those weeds to build carbon and support the health of the elderberry, persimmon, aronia, dogwoods, herbs, and native wildflowers we planted. These images show the progression from barren to bountiful using these weed-free gardening ideas with a focus on increasing carbon in soil. Our landscape can now support so many lush plants that you can't even tell it's the same landscape.

Red clover can be considered a persistent weed in some gardens. In your weed-free garden, it might make a perfect free source of green manure.

As you collect the red clover stems into a bunch around the crown, will you harvest it as free green manure and let it keep growing or pull it out completely?

GO NO- OR LOW-TILL WITH WEEDS

Most people think no-till just means not turning up the soil prior to planting. However, collectively over the gardening year, we can end up doing extensive tilling by ripping out weeds. Remember that example I gave about the scale of our perspective on soil being like seeing the Earth from outer space? Well, on that scale, pulling a single mature weed is like having a small town ripped off the face of the Earth. It's cataclysmic to the residents and has lingering effects through the adjacent areas.

Sometimes, for the health of your existing plants, you may need to pull weeds. For most weeds, though, cutting them to the ground and smothering them with their own leaf matter will slow them down while your plants grow in. That won't kill them, but it limits tilling while feeding the soil more carbon and returning the nutrients the weeds borrowed.

To force weeds to time out with this method, you'll have to repeat the process frequently. As you do, though, each cutting of leaves increases the carbon in your soil. Those cut leaves are literally free carbon that will feed your soil life and benefit your plants.

Garlic is planted in the fall under 2 to 4 inches (5 to 10 cm) of soil and roots deeper in the soil profile to start. My harvests are much larger when I cut weeds as green manure than when I uproot them.

If you can catch weeds when they first germinate, pulling them before they root makes good sense. However, once they've connected with the soil network, using them as a short-term supply of green manure until they die can make your plants grow even better. Still, beware of those rhizomatic stem spreaders and tuber makers we talked about in Part 1 (see page 61). They usually warrant preventative pulling, even when you otherwise practice minimal disturbance gardening to increase carbon.

COMPOST WITH WEEDS

In Part 2 we covered how to make thermophilic compost that will heat-kill or damage weed seeds. But when weeds are super seedy or rhizomatic stem spreaders, I use two other options to make them safe to put back in the garden as a carbon source.

Solarize weeds to make them safe to add to your compost or use under mulch in your garden.

WEED WHACK!

SOLARIZE THOSE GUYS

Solarizing is the process of putting clear plastic on soil to heat it to kill fungal pathogens. Clear plastic is used because it allows light through and encourages the plants below to continue to grow. However, since the plastic cover reduces oxygen and deprives the soil of water, the plants growing below will quickly use the air and flip the soil to anaerobic. Then anaerobic bacteria start to decompose all the dead or dying matter in the soil. Between the plants spending all that energy to stay alive, the bacterial activity that triggers it, and the heat generated by plastic being exposed to sun, the soil gets really hot. After several months, fungal pathogens die.

Unless you also need to eradicate a massive fungal pathogen issue, I don't recommend solarizing the garden as a method to kill weeds. It's considered a last resort because it's so detrimental to soil networks that it can take years to get things back on track. However, I do recommend you solarize harvested weeds if you're concerned they'll survive the compost pile.

Collect all your cut seedy weed tops or stem spreaders into a large, clear plastic bag. Push the air out of the bag and seal it. Then put the bag in a sunny, hot location for a few months. You can even set these bags right on top of weedy areas to use them for suppression of other weeds. Just leave space between the bags so air and water can filter down to the soil below.

Note that there's a huge difference, from a soil perspective, between solarization and light suppression. By using the bags on the soil, you are blocking light to the weeds below. However, because the soil still gets plenty of access to air and moisture, you are not using the plants below to suck oxygen out of the soil and completely alter the habitat below for soil life. There are minor impacts to soil networks right below the bag. However, the area will recover in days, not years, once the bag is moved.

In a few months, the plant matter will look like dark soil. At that point you can add it to your compost pile and then age it before applying to the soil.

Can the compost and use seedy, persistent weeds for natural decomposition in a buried can instead.

Jimsonweed (*Datura stramonium*) is also called thornapple for its large, spiked seed pods. It is a perfect candidate for the weed can. Historically, it was used to help with asthma, though now it's known to be toxic.

WEED WHACK!

CAN THE COMPOST

Another way to decompose weeds without letting them spread is in a buried metal trash can. Start by drilling ½-1 inch drainage holes in the bottom of the can. Then, dig the can into the soil using the same method for digging in an olla (see page 65).

Put a layer of cardboard on the bottom of the can to cover the holes temporarily. As you cut weeds that aren't fit for compost, pile them in the can. Add at a few inches (approximately 7.5 cm) of weeds at a time so they start to smother each other. Also, leave the can open so rain filters to the bottom and out the drainage holes below. Once you fill this to the top, put the lid on for a couple of days so those weeds don't creep back. Then you can open it again and start adding new matter whenever there's room.

Grow perennial plants around the can so the weeds feed those plants and distribute water deeper down in the soil. Just leave yourself a path for easy access.

This works with risky weeds because even if soil life moves those seeds into the soil using the drainage holes, they'll be too deep to germinate. Also, stem spreaders can't seem to find the drainage holes below since they are adapted to run sideways around obstacles.

Note: This isn't a hot or anaerobic composting method. Don't use this can to layer browns and greens. No kitchen scraps, mulch, or cultivated plant debris should go in there. This is a green weed can only. Weedy plant material has the right ratio of green-to-brown all on its own. Plus, those fast growers decompose more quickly than our cultivated plants that put more energy into prettier foliage. That makes them uniquely qualified for this process.

WEED WHACK!

INTENTIONAL COMPACTION

To make an easy weed-free path to access your weed can, consider intentional compaction.

Generally, we want to avoid compacting soil so it can sustain soil life and plants. But intentional compaction is a good tool to keep weeds from spreading to new areas. You only need to compact a 1- to 2-foot (30- to 60-cm) perimeter around a weedy area to slow weed spread.

Use a tamper to compact the soil. Walk on the compaction zone as often as you can.

Mow new growth to the ground each time it starts. Tamp again after rains if it turns mushy. Within a few months of treating soil this terribly, it will become an impermeable barrier that even weeds are slow to cross.

Going forward, to keep it compacted, sweep off organic matter, keep up with mowing, and walk the area whenever you can.

BIOCHAR PRODUCTION

Biochar is a soil amendment made from dried green matter that is turned into charcoal using a low oxygen burning process called pyrolysis. The particular particle structure that results from the burning process creates a stable form of carbon that holds water and nutrients, much like mycorrhizae or humus does.

It's easy to make biochar, even in an urban or suburban backyard, using a Japanese cone kiln. You can make your own cone kiln using sheet metal and rivets or you can buy one online. They look a bit like a backyard firepit. However, their deep conical shape controls the rate of oxygen flow.

These blackberry bull canes are an eyesore when they shoot up in summer. Wear leather gloves and use quality pruning shears to cut through their thick stems to make biochar feedstock.

You can also just dig a conical-shaped hole in the ground to use as a firepit. However, that will damage the soil in the surrounding area and stir up weeds.

WEED WHACK!

MAKE BIOCHAR FROM WEEDS

Lots of weedy materials make perfect feedstocks for biochar. My favorites are the non-fruiting bull canes that our native blackberries send out after the fruit starts ripening. I also use all the canes from the wineberries (*Rubus phoenicolasius*) since it's a non-native invasive in my area.

Harvest the still-living woody materials and cut them into uniform lengths that will fit in the base of your cone kiln. Dry them completely before use.

MAKE BIOCHAR

To make biochar, put a shovel of dry dirt in the bottom of your cone kiln to seal air-gaps, if it's not welded.

Layer on some kindling with your biochar feedstock and start a fire just as you would a backyard firepit. Once the fire gets burning, add as much feedstock as you can without putting the fire out. Keep this going at a low burn (like you do a charcoal grill). Add more feedstock until your cone is about two-thirds full.

Let the materials burn until they look like charcoal. Then douse them with water to put the fire out.

Dry the biochar. Then put it in a heavy-duty bag, like a woven polypropylene feedbag, and crush it by driving over it or using a mallet. The smaller your pieces, the better for your garden.

Optional: To supercharge your biochar, soak it in compost tea that's been spiked with mycorrhizal inoculant before applying to the garden.

APPLYING BIOCHAR

Biochar is powerful stuff. It may temporarily spike your soil pH when applied. However, within a few months it will stabilize again. There are no standardized guidelines for applications in home gardens. However, adding about ½ inch (1 cm) to the top of soil and working it in about 4 to 6 inches (10 to 15 cm) is a good place to start. You can apply biochar annually in poor soil. As conditions improve, cut back to every other year until your soil is officially loam.

CONTROL EROSION

The final carbon farming–related recommendation that can be adapted for your garden is erosion control. Rivers and waterways have to be dredged frequently because carbon-rich soil materials run off into the water. There they accumulate heavy metals and other pollutants that make them unsafe for use in soil. So, all that carbon-rich soil just ends up being managed as toxic waste in specialized landfills.

Most people think of soil erosion as something that happens on steep slopes. but driving rains and winds will cause erosion anywhere soil is not held in place by plant roots. Growing weeds can prevent erosion while capturing carbon as they grow. But again, rather than letting weeds grow out of control, use them strategically as a cover crop.

WEED WHACK!

LET THEM GROW, THEN MOW

Weeds are like rechargeable batteries with a built-in charger. If you mow them down, they use their energy reserves in the roots to grow new leaves. Then they use those new leaves to store energy in the roots again. If you want them to keep regrowing so you get more carbon-rich leaves, then only mow them as often as you need to in order to prevent them from seeding and spreading.

When you're ready to plant with something other than weeds, stop letting them recharge their batteries. To do that, mow them as close to the ground as you can get them. Then, mow them again each time they put on new leaves. If you can take off part of the crown with each mowing that will speed things up further. Some plants may make multiple heads after crown damage, but repeated mowing will still eventually do them in.

On the next page you'll find some of my favorite tools for this method.

If you are mowing to kill, then remember to do it anytime new leaves start. If you can't keep up with the mowing, then cover the area with something that blocks light, such as black plastic sheeting, until you can get back to mowing.

TOOL BAR

This curved blade is designed for grains in a garden. But it will do the job on green stemmed weeds too. For woody weeds, upgrade to a scythe with a ditch blade or use your pruning shears or loppers.

This is an Austrian scythe with a curved blade and a straight handle. American scythes have a curved handle and a straight blade.

THE SICKLE

The sickle is a small-curved knife, often used to harvest grains by hand. It also makes a great weed mower for small areas. Sickles come in different sizes and shapes, depending on use. The standard gardener's sickle is great for most young weeds. If you have a lot of clumping grasses, though, a grain sickle is better.

You'll need to get on the ground to use this for mowing close to the root zone. So, it's not a great option for large areas or for gardeners who don't love bending.

THE SCYTHE

A scythe is like a big sickle that you can use from a standing position. It's a wonderful, low-tech mowing tool for larger areas. Some scythe models allow you to switch the blade for various weed types. Use a grass blade for soft-stemmed plants, a ditch blade for plants with semi-woody stems, and a bush blade for woody stemmed weeds.

Sharpen the blade with a wet stone after every few strokes on tough weeds. They also don't work well for weeds over ½ inch (1 cm) in diameter without excessive, fatiguing force.

TOOL BAR

My string trimmer made quick work of the weeds in this area. Just be very careful not to accidentally hit your trees or other preferred plants or it will make quick work of them, too.

A folding handsaw is a perfect garden tool for cutting through shrubby weeds.

STRING TRIMMER

The string trimmer, also called a weed whacker, weed eater, whipper snipper, or weed trimmer, is a gas- or battery-powered answer to the scythe. Rather than change blades, you change string line width to match your mowing needs. These are excellent for mowing right down to the crown of many weeds.

Sadly, they also spit out bits of string line into your soil as they mow. You can find models with metal blades. Like the scythe, though, the blades wear out quickly and need to be sharpened or replaced. That also makes them heavier. Sometimes you can also find organic string line that's not plastic.

When using these motorized trimmers, wear long-sleeved shirts and pants, gloves, and protective eyewear for safety. They fling a lot of debris. Also, don't use them on weeds with seed heads or it will fling the seeds everywhere.

HANDSAWS, HEDGE TRIMMERS, AND CHAINSAWS

For woody plants, such as shrubs or trees, you'll need to cut through trunks and large branches. You can use manual or motorized hedge trimmers to clear out the greenery to see the trunks or access the branches. Then use handsaws or chainsaws for cutting the branches and trunks down to ground level.

The exact combination of tools you need will depend on the plant and your stamina. Our ancient ancestors did this by hand with primitive tools. Personally, though, I upgrade to a chainsaw for anything more than 3 inches (7.5 cm) thick or if there's a lot of limbs and trunks to cut through.

WEED-FREE GARDENING

WEED WHACK!

POND LINER POWER

To kill weeds with less work after mowing, use a pond liner. These are heavy duty and will only require a few bricks or rocks to hold them in place. They are also UV resistant so they won't decompose in your soil quickly the way cheaper black plastic sheeting will. That means you can use them over and over again to suppress weeds as you expand your garden.

For best results, leave them in place over your weed area from spring to fall. Then, apply cardboard and compost to recharge soil life in winter. Start with a cover crop in spring to make sure the weeds are really controlled.

No digging or regular mowing required when you use pond liner and time to deprive weeds of life by light deprivation.

Carbon-Saving Weed Uses

Using weeds to sink carbon is my idea of a good time. But you can also use weeds to cut down on your use of other resources at home. Many are edible, medicinal, or great for use in garden projects. Here are a few of the ways I use weeds to cut carbon costs in other ways on our homestead.

FERMENTS

A lot of edible weeds are so high in mineral content that they're perfect for fermenting into a tangy, sour, and spicy kimchi-esque condiment. Use this as a nutritious flavor enhancer on other foods. Put a forkful on tacos. Top your burgers with a little in lieu of lettuce. Stir a spoonful into eggs just after you turn off the heat.

Weedy trees, branches, and vines can be used to make trellises in the garden.

GARDEN DECORATIONS

Weedy, fast-growing trees like the wild offspring of the Bradford pear (*Pyrus calleryana*), the Princess Tree (*Paulownia tomentosa*), and bamboo have become my go-to sources for things like bean trellises, decorative fences, wattles, and more. By harvesting them regularly for projects, I keep them from having the energy to spread and get a free resource for the garden.

Bamboo is wonderful for decorative fences, trellises, bean poles, and more. Just use care when handling to avoid getting the itches.

BAMBOO

Bamboo is considered an incredible renewable resource in many parts of the world where it is used for making decorations, furniture, and even housing. However, in places like where I live on the East Coast of the United States, it's just treated like a hard-to-control weed once it gets going. That's because, here, people plant it as a fast-growing privacy screen or for tropical appeal not realizing that it's essentially a rhizome-spreading grass.

If you have an existing stand, you can slow it down considerably by eating the new shoots that emerge from the rhizomes in spring. Then, you can also harvest the mature shoots to use for garden projects or chip for mulch.

WEED WHACK!

MULCH BAMBOO

To make bamboo mulch, use a wood chipper to chip up shoots that are about 1 to 2 inches (2.5 to 5 cm) in diameter. Dry the mulch completely, such as on a tarp in the sun. Turn a few times to make sure it is 100 percent dry. Then, bag this up and wait several months prior to use, as a precaution. Finally, use a light layer of 1 to 2 inches (2.5 to 5 cm) of this under perennial plants as a source of long-term silica.

Some people believe silica boosts plant cell wall strength and makes plants more resilient during weather extremes. Unfortunately, it also makes bamboo slice like blades of itchy grass when handled. So, gear up and use gloves when working with bamboo. And don't put this where you plan to walk barefoot or garden without gloves.

WATTLE AWAY YOUR WEEDS

Wattles are woven branches and stems used for garden beds, fences, or other decorative purposes. They probably started as a practical way to make use of weedy shrubs or coppicing trees to keep pests like pigs and cattle out of the garden beds. Today, though, they add old world charm to gardens. Just make sure you dry any parts that will have contact with soil before you install or they might grow into more weedy trees.

The dog fennel wattle next to the pallet keeps my ducks out of the garden.

WEED WHACK!

TRELLIS UP

Store-bought trellises are expensive and often wear out quickly in the garden. Make our own using coppiced weedy trees with just a few minutes of work.

SUPPORT YOUR HEALTH

Herbal medicine has been used to promote well-being since even before humans began farming. A simple place to start is with topically applied herbs. For example, broadleaf plantain (*Plantago major*) can be crushed and applied to wasp stings to alleviate the itch. Yarrow (*Achillea millefolium*) can be applied to stop bleeding and expedite healing on minor cuts.

When you're ready to ingest medicinal herbs, teas or infusions are an easy place to start. Maypop (*Passiflora incarnata*) leaves and flowers, harvested fresh and boiled in water, make a terrible-tasting, but fantastically soporific tea before bed. Dried mugwort (*Artemisia vulgaris*) leaves make for a mood-improving, fragrant, bitter tea.

When you start learning about the historical uses of weeds, you'll find lots of ways to save money while sinking carbon in your garden.

In healthy soil, broadleaf plantain (*Plantago major*) grows big, beautiful leaves and can stand in for hostas. I grow it under my hazelnut trees since deer don't eat it.

There are many edible weeds that can be made into a salad or fermented.

This vining passionflower vine is a native weed that produce inedible, seed-filled fruit in my area. But its leaves make an incredible sleep-aiding infusion.

BETTER LIVING WITH WEEDS

I love to talk weeds with famous gardeners. I'm always surprised at how many of the people who inspire us to be better gardeners have not just a healthy respect for weeds, but downright appreciation for them, too. Let me share a few weed-free gardening perspectives from three garden influencers you likely know and love.

MISILLA DELA LLANA shares her family legacy and love of gardening with daily doses of extremely practical, well-researched information and inspiration on Instagram (@learntogrow). She constantly surprises me with the depth and breadth of quality content she shares to make gardening easier for others. She's also the author of the wonderful book *Four-Season Food Gardening*. Here are her weed-free strategies.

"We do not use herbicides as we choose to garden organically. Consistent use may linger for long periods and harm organisms. Potentially harmful chemicals may contaminate the soil and water. Besides digging up weeds, we apply mulches and/or weed barriers to suppress and prevent spreading.

One of Misilla's most loved weeds is wood sorrel (*Oxalis* spp.). She even uses it as ground cover in her garden.

"Although weeding is a task, it can be therapeutic, as well. It is like meditating in the garden. It frees my thoughts and gives me a calm feeling afterwards. That feeling of accomplishment while making the garden neat and beautiful.

"We grow claytonia as part of our perennial edible garden. The flavor reminds me of spinach; it is tasty and succulent. It can be put in salads, soups, and smoothies and can be juiced. It self-seeds, but it's manageable. It can also be grown as a ground cover.

"We love lemon balm due to its medicinal nature. It makes a calming, soothing tea, and can be used for other discomfort. It repels mosquitoes and fungus gnats due to its citronellal content. I rub the leaves on exposed skin when I'm gardening.

"The creeping buttercup is the most noxious weed I have ever encountered. It is prolific and invasive. A self-propagating weed via stolons where buds emerge and root similar to strawberry runners. I usually uproot the whole plant and place it in a compost tumbler (hot compost)."

ASHLIE THOMAS is elegance embodied in the garden. Her octagon beds and she-shed, built with help from her hubby Tyler, are on my "to drool" list. (That's the list of the things I wish I could have once I get done with my actual to-do list.) If you want to see exactly how classy weed-free gardening can be, find her on Instagram (@the.mocha.gardener). Also, check out her book *How to Become a Gardener*. Here are her weed-free strategies.

"My approach to weed management is quite simple in that I strive to work with nature and not against it. What may be considered a nuisance to my garden plans, may in actuality have complex ecological and nutritional benefits for me and other species that I coexist with. Therefore, I focus on growing native plants that can outcompete many of the common weeds and avoiding harsh chemicals, which can inadvertently disrupt the soil microbiome.

"Originating from western Asia and the Mediterranean region, common purslane (*Portulaca oleracea*) is an annual succulent weed found globally. Despite its invasive nature, it is considered a highly nutritious and valuable plant for both wildlife and humans. I love this plant because nearly all parts are edible, and it has the flavor profile of spinach, which makes it more of a benefit than a nuisance.

"Dandelion (*Taraxacum officinale*) is one of my favorite herbs due to some of its chemical components being considered medicinal and nutrient dense. I enjoy pulling dandelions from the root, as all parts are delicious in various dishes. When dried, the roots make an excellent bitter tea. Furthermore, young, raw dandelion leaves are refreshing in salads.

"Simply put, crabgrass (*Digitaria*) is the bane of my existence, and I am sure that other gardeners would agree. Nevertheless, crabgrass in isolation is quite aesthetically pleasing with its flat, deep green blades. This low-profile annual weed typically emerges in the summer and thrives in warm weather, and, due to its drought-tolerant characteristic, it has the ability to withstand high temperatures

Ashlie's has a few weeds in her garden. But with all that lush growth all around, they basically blend in.

with little water. I work to eradicate this weedy grass whenever it appears in the garden in our yard, as its crab-like features can quickly compete against intentional plants for space and nutrients."

NIKI JABBOUR is the award-winning author of the extremely popular book *The Year-Round Vegetable Gardener.* Her latest book, *Growing Under Cover: Techniques for a More Productive, Weather-Resistant, Pest-Free Vegetable Garden*, is awesome. She's from Halifax, Nova Scotia, and you can find her on Instagram (@nikijabbour). She's also one of the power trio responsible for the amazing website SavvyGardening.com.

Given all the great writing she does, I can't believe Niki has time to garden at all. But somehow, she finds ways to pursue all her passions while also inspiring us. Here are her weed-free strategies.

Even in Niki's well-managed, raised vegetable beds a few weeds find their way in (and back out as a delicious bonus greens harvest).

"Not all weeds are bad news. I love finding purslane in my garden beds—and actually plant cultivated purslane in my summer garden for a bumper crop of the heat-tolerant greens. They make a delicious salad green when dressed simply with olive oil, lemon juice, and a sprinkle of salt.

"Unfortunately, I've got a couple of tenacious weeds around the perimeter of my raised bed vegetable garden, all thanks to 'pass-along plants' given to me by well-meaning friends. And while they're not technically growing in my beds, I don't want them to wander that way, so I've been trying to eradicate them. Field bindweed came in a clump of daylilies and is trying its best to gain a foothold in my garden. Goutweed arrived in a pot of hosta and it's been an ongoing struggle to contain its spread. If left to grow, it quickly creates a dense carpet of foliage that chokes out other plants.

"In my vegetable garden my weedy philosophy is simple: weed smart and I approach the task with three tactics: 1. I pull weeds as soon as I spot them (this means learning to ID weeds in an immature stage). 2. NEVER let weeds go to seed (they'll haunt you for years to come). 3. Mulch is your best friend. Mulching with straw or shredded leaves is an easy way to subdue weeds with several side benefits: increased soil moisture and a reduction of soilborne diseases like early blight."

PART FOUR

CREATING PEACE IN THE GARDEN

Any place you consider your garden is your domain. You get to choose the plants and the aesthetics that appeal most to you. It's also where you should expect to spend extra time filling niches or controlling weeds if you opt not to fill them. Yet, within your garden, by working towards those long-term natural and beneficial soil improvement goals of better drainage, more organic matter, increased mycorrhizal connections, and more plants to sink carbon, your garden can become a place for easy, pleasurable gardening without constantly battling weeds.

Your garden design, your decorative choices, and the plants you choose to grow can also help make your garden healthier while having a big impact on our shared environment. Frankly, though, the days of filling our landscapes with plants that serve no ecological purpose is becoming less fashionable. Now, the trend is towards thriving, diverse landscapes designed to support wildlife, remove carbon from the atmosphere, and nourish us in multiple ways.

If you run and play on your lawn or spread out a blanket and picnic on them as a way of life, then perhaps you do want a lawn. Rather than a single species C3 lawn, adding in mini-clover, low growing flower bulbs, and some mixed seasonal grasses will be just as useful and beautiful. If you aren't using your lawn, then maybe a micro prairie or meadow might be more weed-free.

> "Your garden can become a place for easy, pleasurable gardening without constantly battling weeds."

These aren't no maintenance gardens, but they are lower-maintenance than conventional lawns. Plus, when weedy plants happen, they don't stick out like an unmowed eyesore.

As Kelly D. Norris puts it so eloquently in his stunning book *New Naturalism: Designing and Planning a Resilient, Ecologically Vibrant Home Garden*, "[w]eeding, pruning, and cutting back are editorial gestures that adjudicate the trajectory of a garden." Doesn't that sound a lot less stressful than mowing multiple times per week to maintain a monoculture?

A cottage garden lends itself to letting a few weeds be part of the broader picture.

Personally, as an Epicurean homesteader, edible landscapes and ornamental farming are my bailiwick. Integrating the food production aspects of having a vegetable garden or orchard with the ornamental aspects of more structured, decorative landscapes that I loved from my time in France are my passion. Food is beautiful, not just on our plates, but also in our landscapes. Lush carpets of varied colored come and cut lettuces crowd out weeds while looking lovely. A pumpkin patch running around a traditional container urn hide my complete failure to weed during the writing of this book!

Perennial foods, grown in carbon-rich soil, require hardly any maintenance and have their own weed prevention methods built in. My horseradish that starts in March and ends in December looks like a hedge with smartweed ground cover keeping its roots cool and protected. My long-flowering fennel stuns from late winter to late summer when I harvest its seeds. It doesn't mind a bit that dollarweed sends insignificant rhizome snakes amid its roots. Both of these plants shade and outcompete weeds with their early start and late finish.

In an edible landscape, I don't have to weed the way I would with perfectly spaced rows. When I mix annuals with perennials there's never a moment when a bed is completely empty and open for weeds. Perennial herbs are fantastic for pollinators, too. Hedges of lavender or rosemary are easy to grow in well-draining soil and moderate climates. Mints can grow as lush as grass in good soil, and they smell so much better when you mow them. Basils come in tons of leaf colors and can even be grown for giant flower heads. When you intermix those like a patchwork and weeds grow between, no one even notices. They just add other leaf or flower textures to the eclectic display.

My garden looks like a mulch display for a couple of weeks in late winter before all my plantings take off. But this is how I control weeds and rapidly improve soil to save work in the long-term.

Food forests are a wilder, more direct mimicry of nature than a designed edible landscape. But they also have their beauty. More importantly, though, weeding becomes completely unnecessary. No weed can compete with my native pawpaw, grapevine, blackberry, lemon balm, and red perilla plant guild. That's interplanting at its finest and the easiest way I know to grow food.

No matter what type of garden you favor, though, you need to focus on carbon capture with dense plantings and continuous soil improvement. Otherwise, nature will keep sending weeds to fill that niche. In less fertile soils, that can be hard to do. Mixing and matching mulches, using containers on the beds, and other methods can fill spaces that nature wants to fill with weeds. As your soil improves and your plants become radiantly healthy, then they'll appreciate more company.

Kick-Start Carbon Cycling

Let's get into the garden with a closer look at ways to utilize and adapt some popular weed-free methods to kick-start the carbon cycling when making new garden beds.

SQUARE FOOT GARDENING

Mel Bartholomew started a gardening revolution with his square foot gardening method. You begin by building a raised bed frame divisible by square feet such as a 4 x 4-foot (1.2 x 1.2-m) bed. Cover the area inside and under the edges of the bed with cardboard to suppress the grass by light deprivation. Then, fill that bed frame with 6 inches (15 cm) of soilless planting mix. Frankly, that's a perfect formula for short-term weed prevention of any full sun–loving plant or lawn. Also, since the beds are square or rectangular, they're easier to mow around than odd shapes.

Mel's planting mix is also genius. Peat moss is used for good drainage and to give nutrients something to bind to, so they don't wash away. Technically, peat counts as organic matter. However, it's so slow to decompose it can stay in the bed for years, acting like a stable sponge for nutrients. That also gives it temperature stabilizing effects because it not as biologically active as other organic matter. (Peat moss may not be sustainable in some areas. Finely shredded leaf compost works as a substitute.)

Coarse vermiculite is also added for its amazing ability to bond with water molecules without becoming boggy. The coarse size creates larger air spaces for soil life to thrive and roots to spread. Vermiculite technically counts as inorganic matter (like rocks). However, the small particle size and moisture retention qualities encourage faster shedding of trace minerals that plants can use. That makes it a bit of a mineral source, too.

The final ingredient is a blend of as many different kinds of compost you can find. By using more than one type, you offset the risks of a bad batch contaminating your bed. You also increase the likelihood of well-balanced nutrients and microlife for plant health. Also, the low pH of the peat offsets the high pH of many store-bought composts. The net result is a well-draining, ideal pH, nutrient-rich, and weed-free planting medium.

Plant spacing guidelines are based on square feet, such as sixteen carrots, nine turnips, or two corn stalks per square foot (30 square cm). That keeps the area sufficiently stocked to suppress breakthrough weeds from below. You're also encouraged to mix and match your squares so your bed isn't a monoculture.

The final bit of brilliance of Mel's system is that, at the end of the year, you pack up your raised bed frame and rake out the planting mix. Then, you start the system in a new location the following year. Unfortunately, people who skip that step and top the beds off with garden soil instead have disastrous results, including weed invasions the following year. Since compost is what gets used in the bed first, backfilling with garden soil makes the bed peat and vermiculite heavy with few nutrients. The pH also trends acidic with no compost to buffer it.

TOOL BAR

"The gardener did it in the garden with the dibber" ought to be an option in the game Clue. This adorably named ice pick-like tool pokes through dead roots to start seedlings with less soil disturbance.

THE DIBBER

To make room for new seedlings during transplanting or direct planting, hold the handle between your fingers and plunge the dibber tip into the earth. Move the tip in a circular motion to widen the planting hole. Remove the dibber carefully so the hole stays open. Drop in your transplants and compress the soil slightly. Or, fill the hole with seed starting mix and drop in some seeds to give seedlings a quick start.

If you want to leave this bed in place to plant again, grow an overwintering cover crop. Mow that down in spring. Smother it with a few layers of newspaper. Then, top the bed off to the rim with fresh, aged compost. Use the same spacing as before, but rotate your crops so you don't get pests and pathogens.

To sow seeds or plug in plant starts, use the dibber to poke through paper.

Also, plan weed prevention around the sides of the bed since those will get weedy in year two. Another alternative is to remove the bed and leave the mix in place. Then use the area to plant a diverse mix of perennial fruits, flowers, and evergreen herbs in fall. After planting, cover the bed with a 1- to 2-inch (2.5- to 5-cm) layer of loose leaf or wood mulch to suppress weed seeds stirred up by digging.

This works well because the planting mix that remains is mostly made up of slow decomposing materials like peat, vermiculate, and a little compost to act as mulch. Plus, since perennials root in deeper soil, they won't be bothered by the slightly acidic pH in the planting mix. If the soil below was growing grass before, then it's likely already in the right pH range for growing fruits (except blueberries). The decomposing grass buried below becomes a slow-release nitrogen source where weeds can't find it. Going forward, since perennials don't need a lot of nitrogen, focus on fall-applied high-carbon mulches just before the old materials break down.

STRAW BALE GARDENING

Straw bale gardening, made famous by Joel Karsten's *Straw Bale Gardens Complete*, revolutionized the way

In my trials, fall-planted white Sonora wheat had a major allelopathic and soil occupancy advantage over bare soil. The right side of the image is with wheat, and the left is what happened in bare soil.

we think about gardening. Suddenly, gardeners everywhere realized that you don't need soil or premade potting mix to garden. You just need organic matter, water, fertilizer, and some hyped-up microlife to make your own.

Since straw is also wonderful short-term mulch for weed seed suppression, creating a straw bale garden over a weedy area is a fantastic way to kick-start short-term weed prevention. Wheat straw even has minor allelopathic abilities that work as it decays.

The standard practice for conditioning straw bales uses nitrogen-based, synthetic lawn fertilizer not ideal for organic weed-free gardening. That fast-acting fertilizer can filter down to the soil below and trigger weeds. So, I don't recommend it. But Joel also offers an organic solution more suitable for weed-free gardening.

The budget-conscious homesteader in me has to tell you that 1 part fresh urine (a rich nitrogen source) diluted with 10 parts water works well to kick-start straw bale decomposition. Start with that, then follow Joel's schedule of fertilizer applications using just 1 cup (235 ml) of organic fertilizer with a "5" in the nitrogen position, such as 5-3-2 (N-P-K), per application. Also, water the bales with vermicompost tea or other organic liquid fertilizer during conditioning and while plants are growing to encourage bacterial activity.

This straw bale garden uses weed mats under and around the bales as weed prevention. This won't increase carbon in the soil. However, it's a perfect way to grow annual vegetables while using light deprivation to kill many existing plants in the ground below.

Used-up straw bale beds can be transitioned into permanent planting beds for perennials in under a year with minimal weeding.

In early spring, start by putting down a few layers of cardboard over an area twice as large as the bales. Cover it with 3 to 4 inches (7.5 to 10 cm) of shredded wood or wood chips. The conditioning process is basically a way to make compost using only fertilizer and straw bales. So, that mulch acts as a buffer for those BODs and phenols I mentioned in Part 3.

After conditioning, move aside some of the decomposing straw. Then drop in some organic potting mix. This is the same concept as with the dibber, only the hole is larger and more plant-starting medium is used. After this you can grow vegetables and herbs in these beds.

THE NO-WORK GARDENING METHOD

About eight to ten weeks before your first frost, rake what's left of the bales over the surface of your mulch area at depth of about 3 to 4 inches (7.5 to 10 cm) thick. Plant a cover crop of hard winter wheat (hardy down to -15°F [-26°C]). The wheat will grow through the composted straw and mulch in the soil below to help integrate. It will also help integrate these layers and utilize the leftover nutrients that would otherwise encourage weeds.

Let the wheat grow until late spring, then mow down the stalks and leave the roots in place. After that, spread some paper and cover it with 1 to 2 inches (2.5 to 5 cm) of aged compost. Then you can use that area for in-ground vegetables. Grow late-season heavy feeders (okra, tomatoes) that don't require soil disturbance the first year. Alternatively, you can also grow two rounds of cover crops like tillage radish, mowed and left in place, followed by millet or buckwheat.

This method is a high-nitrogen kick-start that needs to be heavily planted for at least a full year after the bales decompose. But it's a very effective way to get a lot of carbon in the soil quickly. When the soil just looks like lovely dark loam, then transition this to a perennial planting area with mulch or paper followed by compost using the same methods covered under square foot gardening (see page 148).

Ruth Stout was an organic gardener who grew a large vegetable garden without tilling into her eighties. In collaboration with Richard Clemence, Ruth's collected articles on organic gardening were compiled into a book called *The Ruth Stout No-Work Garden Book: Secrets of the Year-Round Mulch Method*; this book still has tremendous impact today.

The basis of her method was simply to garden in mulch. Ruth recommended starting with about 8 inches (20 cm) of old hay. But she surmised that straw, leaves, pine needles, sawdust, and any vegetative matter that eventually decomposes might work. Ruth noted in her book that she had sandy soil and no experience with other soil types.

After mulching, move the mulch aside to start plants in the soil. Hill up the mulch around the plant stems as they grow. If weeds happen, fold them down and cover them with more mulch. Leave plant residues not harvested as mulch. Flatten deceased plants to the ground in winter and cover with another 4 to 5 inches (10 to 13 cm) of mulch over the whole area. Keep doing this every year for as long as you garden in that area.

I've used this system many times in clay soil with a variety of different mulch materials with varying results. Here are some recommendations on how to use the different types.

HAY/GRASS

In my experience, hay bales are either full of weed seeds or full of herbicide residues. That makes them not ideal for weed-free organic gardening. However, cut grass has a similar nutrient profile to hay. It's just not dried. You can use it instead of hay if it hasn't been heavily sprayed with herbicides.

Because it's full of moisture, it will hot compost if you apply 8 inches (20 cm) of it at a time. So, instead layer on a few inches (approximately 7.5 cm) at a time, such as when you mow, until you've put on the full 8 inches (20 cm). This only worked for three years in my soil, though, before plants started to stunt from nutrient overload. I consider it a good way to start a bed before transitioning it to compost.

Straw on its own didn't pack the power punch necessary for hungry vegetables. Once mixed with some manure, though, it works fantastic. I add extra straw in my chicken and goat areas in late summer and fall. Then I harvest their litter back out as my mulch. I put it on in mid-winter, then plant in late spring so pathogens time out.

This is my favorite medium for tomatoes, sesame, sunflowers, corn, and other plants that don't grow in direct contact with the ground. I also time applications for dry periods or cover it with a tarp during rain to keep it from becoming mucky.

My variation of the no-work method uses litter from my livestock areas. You can see how well that suppresses weeds compared to the prolific growth all around.

PINE NEEDLES

Pine needles don't decompose quickly, so organic fertilizer is needed when using them for vegetables. Using the prescribed 8 inches (20 cm) is hard to garden in, but 4 to 6 inches (10 to 15 cm) is fine. The weeds that do poke through need to be cut since pine needles aren't heavy enough to weight them down.

Overall, I can't recommend pine needles for vegetables, but it's wonderful for blueberries and azaleas in low pH soils.

LEAVES

Whole leaves as a mulch for new beds are also difficult to garden in. Finely mulched leaves are incredible for clay, though. They get incorporated into soil quickly, so you may need to apply more than once a year. They are lower in nutrients than hay or straw and manure. For hungry plants, slow-release organic fertilizer was still necessary. Long-term use of mulched leaf beds has proven to be the least weedy of all the mulches I've trialed.

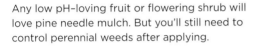

Any low pH–loving fruit or flowering shrub will love pine needle mulch. But you'll still need to control perennial weeds after applying.

This new garden area is a no-work mulch garden. I used leaf mulch for the planting area and double-shredded hardwood for the paths. The paper below is painter paper from the hardware store.

OTHER DETAILS

This method only prevents weeds if you keep using it forever. Stop gardening in that area for a month, and it's a weed field. Forget to mulch one year and your soil will rebel by sending weeds. Also, since this is lots of organic matter all at once, using taprooted crops as often as you can will help work it in faster.

WOOD MULCH GARDENING

Several years ago, I watched a heartwarming documentary about a master arborist and gardener named Paul Gautschi. He credits God with revealing the wisdom of what's now called back to Eden gardening.

Paul's process is to put down about 4 inches (10 cm) of arborist mulch on top of soil. Then, like Ruth, he moves back the mulch to plant and hills it up around the plants as they grow. Paul says in the video that weeds are easily raked out. Every few years, when the material

is decomposed, he spreads more arborist mulch to renew the soil. He also uses chicken manure for fertilizer.

Arborist mulch typically includes a mix of chipped, rather than shredded, hardwoods and softwoods and some leaves. Those qualities mean it's better draining than shredded hardwoods. Also, the mix of various-size branches, stems, and leaves encourages speedier decomposition to make nutrients available to plants right away. Electric companies often give wood away for free. However, they also regularly spray the areas and trees they cut with herbicides. Getting it from an arborist or making your own is better.

Aptly referred to as dog vomit, this slime mold (*Fuligo septica*) is a common occurrence after large applications of wood mulch.

My trials resulted in a huge outbreak of dog vomit slime mold, followed by blewits, a pH of 8.0, and severely stunted plants in year one. But in the second year, the soil was a fantastic place to grow all sorts of woody perennial herbs. This also makes the easiest-to-weed soil.

I should note that Paul grows his vegetables in the rain shadow of the Olympic mountains in Washington where average rainfall is about 16 inches (41 cm) per year. In most places that would qualify as desert. But frequent fog, regular cool breezes, and the mollisols soils, which are high in humic content and retain lots of moisture, make his region ideal for perennial grasslands, slow-growth forests, and lavender farms. I suspect that, like Ruth's method, this is amazing for sandy, well-draining soils.

LAYERED BED-MAKING

In *The Complete Guide to No-Dig Gardening*, Charlie Nardozzi offers a simple and really effective layered bed-making recipe that starts with cutting the grass or weeds and topping it with five or six overlapped layers of wet newspaper or cardboard. Then, top that with a 3- to 4-inch-thick (7.5- to 10-cm) layer of green,

or high nitrogen, organic materials such as fresh grass clippings, seaweed, kitchen scrap veggies, or seed- and root-free weeds. Next comes a 1- to 2-inch (2.5- to 5-cm) thick layer of compost, followed by a 3- to 4-inch (7.5- to 10-cm) thick layer of carbon (brown) material such as straw, chopped leaves, shredded paper, sawdust, or hay.

This is essentially a compost pile made where you want your new gardening bed to be. This process is also called sheet mulching or lasagna gardening. The formula for the layers can vary based on what materials are available to you. The important thing is to realize this is a compost pile built in place to start a garden bed. The layers need sufficient air circulation and moisture until they fully break down.

In my experience, just like the area around a regular compost pile, this process sets off weed eruptions for about a 5- to 10-foot (1.5- to 3-m) radius around the bed, as leachate encourages more microlife. As a precaution, like with straw bale gardening, I cover an area at least twice the size of the bed with a carbon-rich mulch as a soil buffer and leachate sponge.

Using sprawling plants to shade weeds is a great way to start weed-free, compost-rich garden beds. You can also use it as a control tactic later in a bad weed year.

Also, this is a nutrient-rich way to make a bed. Use this for hungry vegetables for a year or two before you use it for perennials. When the initial compost cover gets integrated into the soil, cover with more aged compost and stay on cover of weedlings.

NO-DIG COMPOST BEDS

Another no-dig gardener, UK-based Charles Dowding, is more specifically aged-compost focused. He and Stephanie Hafferty coauthored a beautiful book called *No Dig Organic Home & Garden*, which also gets into ways to use and store your harvests.

To begin a new bed using Charles's method, apply cardboard followed by any kind of mulch, though compost is favored. Then, you can also follow up with landscape fabric as a light barrier on top of the compost and around the plants for additional weed prevention.

In the first few years, while weed pressure is intense, grow sprawling/shading crops like pumpkin to reduce weeds by limiting light reaching the soil below. Then, at least once a year keep topping the beds

with homemade compost that's aged eight to twelve months. Charles also suggests using other mulches as nutrient sources like seaweed, hay, cut grass, sawdust, and chipped bark if necessary.

If you have soil that contains at least 2 percent organic matter and several inches (approximately 7.5 cm) of depth to begin with, this method works fantastic. Most of my soil had less than 0.5 percent organic matter to begin with, so I start beds using the other methods we just covered. Then, I move on to using just aged compost a few years later.

I also recommend not using composted manure or livestock bedding exclusively. Like regular applications of grass, eventually the soil fatigues of having the same diet every year. Then plants suffer, too.

Grow bags can be used as a weed suppression method or a way to garden above ground in places where the weeds are too problematic to grow in.

GROW BAG GARDENING

Generally, I have strong feelings about the importance of growing in the ground if you are able to. That's the only way plants can sink carbon and relate to soil networks. However, if you have parts of your garden that are just too weedy to grow in, grow bags are an inexpensive way to grow right on top of really weedy areas. Because the bags are permeable but don't have drainage holes, you can even set them on top of areas that are full of rhizomatic spreaders.

If you really want to get deeper into grow bags, then *Grow Bag Gardening: The Revolutionary Way to Grow Bountiful Vegetables, Herbs, Fruits, and Flowers in Lightweight, Eco-friendly Fabric Pots* by Epic Gardening guru Kevin Espiritu is the resource you need. But if you just need

a temporary way to grow potatoes and sweet potatoes while you deal with a weed situation, I have a quick trick.

Fill your bags with leaf compost. Leaf compost is leaf mold that's aged to the point of looking like a fine compost. You'll also have to use some organic vegetable garden fertilizer. But the leaf compost plus fertilizer works out to be a wonderful planting medium. Also, at the end of the year, if you want to dump your grow bags, they make perfect mulch for any of your beds.

Additionally, setting the grow bags right on top of some weeds can smother and deprive them of light, making this another weed suppression option.

Flagstone is harder to keep weed-free than solid, flat surfaces, such as poured concrete patios. Power washing and regular removal of organic matter can reduce weeds.

Pavers set in sand are also weed-prone after a couple of years.

Decorative Decisions

Starting beds is one piece of the puzzle. But gardens aren't just planting beds and plants. They also include all sorts of personal decorative details. Frankly, not all decorative choices are low maintenance on the weed front. So, unless you want to do extra work, then make fewer weed-prone choices.

For example, flagstone is a lovely, natural material that creates a very casual, old world feeling. But all those nooks and crannies collect runoff organic matter and moisture. That makes them particularly weed-prone. Power wash or scrub away the organic matter at least once a year. Then pick weeds as they show up.

Pavers set in sand or mortar can also become weed-prone as organic matter settles in spaces between. These just need to be scraped out and reset periodically. Or you can try to grow things like moss or creeping plants between the spaces to crowd out weeds.

When strawberry runners spill over the edge of this terraced bed I just cut them off with scissors before they root.

This border isn't holding soil or acting as a raised bed. It's just a visual barrier to make it obvious if my *Rosa rugosa* shrub tries to expand into my seating area.

Borders, too, can be a mixed bag when it comes to weed-free gardening. In some situations, they are a perfect place for weeds to get a foothold. In others, they're the perfect tool to keep weedy plants from expanding their territory. I love a decorative border around strawberries and as a visual barrier for stem spreaders, like the *Rosa rugosa* I grow for rose petals and rosehips. But, in new garden areas where weeds are still frequently pushing up in walkways, borders make it hard to weed.

For raised beds, the bed area is almost always less weedy because you fill that space with some kind of container mix that naturally contains fewer weeds. However, the outside edges of the beds are always potential places for weeds to begin.

This weed is taking advantage of the soil from inside the bed and the mulch in the path to get a great start growing.

This wattle lines a walkway, and I encourage the deadnettle to grow along it to give it a cottage-like feel.

Beds made with things like cut trees are a little weedy at first. However, as those materials start to decompose in contact with the soil, they prevent weeds from growing directly under them. Then you just have to worry about weeds that show up in the walkways.

Wider profile permanent materials like concrete blocks or interlocking retaining wall blocks also seem to reduce weeds as they settle into soil. However, cracks between blocks that don't interlock can be a source of weeds.

ROCK MULCHES

Rock mulches can be fantastic tools for promoting drainage around your beds, lowering or raising soil temperature, and aesthetically pleasing weed reduction. They can work in paths, seating areas, or rock gardens. Let's look at some common types.

PEA GRAVEL

Pea gravel is the most common in gardens because it compresses and drains well. It's also nice to walk on. I have to confess, though, I despise it for weed control. The gravel size is so small that they decompose quickly and hold a lot of moisture and organic matter that plants root in. It degrades quickly and needs to be topped off quite frequently. It also only stays put with hard edging and no slope.

These wedges and branches from a cut tree will decompose and act as mulch to help reduce weeds. However, the irregular shapes make it necessary to mow the outer edges with a string trimmer for a close cut. DIY grow bags add decorative interest and weed prevention here too.

Pea gravel is pretty and nice to walk on. It always seems very weed-prone, as shown here where morning glories have taken over after just two months on the ground.

RIVER ROCK

River rock is polished rock that looks like larger-size pea gravel. It's heavier and compresses better than pea gravel, which makes it more weed-resistant. It's lower maintenance overall. But its small size means it's still best to use with edging and on mostly flat areas.

LAVA ROCK

I grew up in Southern California when red lava rock was all the rage in rose gardens. After that, I never wanted to see it in my garden. However, there are lots of different colors and shapes of volcanic rock available. Some are quite pretty. It's top light and can be picked up by winds. It also floats almost as well as bark in heavy rain and on slopes. So, it seems best for flat dry, low wind areas.

CRUSHER RUN

Crusher run is mixed-size rocks that aren't polished. It's most commonly used for driveways. Most people don't prefer it for gardens because it's not as comfortable to walk on. However, from a weed-free perspective, it's my favorite. It compacts better than other sizes. The larger size also seems to drain better and is easier to pull weeds out of. It can also last years without needing to be topped off.

Regardless of the type of rock mulch you choose, you will want to use at least 4 inches (10 cm) to start. Expect to have to rake out weeds.

River rock is a little more weed-resistant and durable than pea gravel and just as pretty.

This Mount Airy North Carolina crusher run granite is fending off the morning glory invasion that took over the pea gravel. It also stays cooler than other rocks due to the light color.

TOOL BAR

GARDEN RAKE

The standard garden rake can be used like a hoe to pull up young weeds or spread amendments. The back can smooth out compost before planting. Claw rakes are perfect for pulling weeds out of rock paths. Leaf rakes collect all that wonderful material that you want for your leaf mold.

The garden rake, claw rake, and leaf rake all make weed control easier in the garden in very different ways.

Lighter colors will also keep your garden cooler. Darker colors will warm up on sunny days and heat the soil below and all around. Rocks also shed minerals and improve drainage, which can make some plants that like dry mineral soils grow better.

ROCK DUST

Rock dust is ground rock that compresses when tamped. People use it in paths. But in my experience, like compost, it needs refreshing every year to keep it weed-free. Otherwise, it quickly becomes a planting medium for certain kinds of weeds.

KEEPING ROCKS IN PLACE

Most rocks are applied over weed mat and lined with edging to hold them in place. Edging is so expensive that I usually just dig the path down below the surface of the soil, tamp it, line it with weed mat, then fill it up just above ground level. This method means that sometimes the soil bleeds into the rocks and makes it weed prone. So, I also grow plants right up to the edge and slightly over into the rocks to outcompete the weeds.

For the lowest maintenance option, use sturdy nonorganic edging with no cracks. Metal overlapped or poured concrete forms are ideal to keep soil from bleeding into rocks and becoming a new planting bed. Materials like wood tend to decay quickly in contact with well-draining rocks. Plan to replace them often for weed control.

This is what the weed-free garden looked like before I mowed. I kept the fruit trees and the *Rosa rugosa* pictured here as the foundation for this new cultivated garden.

The Weed-Free Garden

Now that we've covered some of the different kinds of decisions and options you have when starting or expanding a weed-free gardening area, let's work through an example together.

STEP 1: CHOOSE A LOCATION

While writing this book, I converted the semi-wild space shown in the photo above to a virtually weed-free garden. Do the same in your landscape by identifying the area you want to convert to a weed-free garden.

STEP 2: IDENTIFY, STUDY, AND USE THE WEEDS TO PLAN SOIL PREPARATION TACTICS

Next, I studied the weeds and figured out my strategies for control before I mowed them down. Most of the weeds were annuals like ragweed, broadleaf plantain, grasses, and smartweed taking advantage of open soil, but they weren't problem solving. I knew those would be easy to control by putting down paper and mulch.

The density of curly dock growing on the left-hand side of the bed area helped me identify a drainage problem that needed to be corrected.

I used bamboo to create the bed layout. Then, I put down paper and various mulches, and started some cover crops to begin long-term weed control.

There were some blackberry canes and Oriental bittersweet (*Celastrus orbiculatus*). They had moved in from an adjacent area and weren't very established. I decided it was better to dig them up entirely before they became more established instead of trying to control them later.

There were also a couple areas with large numbers of curly dock (*Rumex crispus*). For those, I decided to control them with mowing and some strategic light deprivation since digging them up would disturb the existing fruit trees. I could also see that their growing area seemed wetter than other parts of the garden. So, I dug a little swale just outside the garden area to slow water down before it hit that point.

STEP 3: GET TO WORK

After that came the fun part of laying out the beds. I live in a rural area with few regulations. So, other than making sure I didn't dig or build beds and a fence over the underground power lines, I got to have some fun with this design.

I used paper, topped with compost, in the center bed. Then I planted those with various mustards, kale, and collards in fall to grow through winter for their mild allelopathic abilities. I also added in some tulip bulbs to pretty up the beds. Bulbs and large tubers can also outcompete many annual weeds since they root deeper in the soil.

The crimson clover and wheat next to the fence help the compost integrate into the soil without upsetting the already established plum tree.

For persistent taprooted curly dock, cover with potted plants or wait until it flowers to cut it back to the ground. I'm using both methods of control in this image.

Cover crops like this mustard don't have to be boring. They just need to be densely planted and be able to grow quickly and stay healthy to keep weeds at bay.

Under the plum tree nearest to our driveway, I wanted to create a terraced bed. However, I needed to do it slowly to avoid triggering the tree to sucker as I added organic matter to level the bed. I've been alternating compost with cover crops in that area and raising the soil bit by bit. I also added in some dahlias to create a big, leafy mass and stunning flowers to make the area feel planted even as I kept working the soil level up.

After mowing the dock and grasses down a few times in the area around the central plum tree, I laid down multiple layers of newspaper near, but not right around, the tree trunk. I covered the grassy half of the bed with leaf mold to plant in. I put heavier double-shredded hardwood on the dock side to suppress them a little longer. Then, I also moved some temporary pots into the dock area to shade the soil and weight down the mulch. Some docks still came through. I let those flower and then cut them again to control.

The paper and mulch took care of almost all of the weeds in the non-dock side of the bed. Then I used some lettuce and nasturtiums as the cover crop for this area.

In the back of the garden, there are a lot of weeds growing around that area. So, I opted to start with a mulch layer over cardboard and some straw bale beds to see what would creep in. One blackberry cane and some false strawberries (*Potentilla indica*) had to be hand-pulled.

These straw bale beds will be used to start in-ground beds in fall.

STEP 4: REEVALUATE

After your first-round planting, it's time to reevaluate to see if any new weeds arrived or if other suppression techniques need to be used. In this garden, there were very few weeds thanks to the materials, cover crops, and techniques used. But we had a particularly hot, dry summer. So, rather than try to start new plants in a stressful situation, I put in a second round of cover crops in two of the beds. Once the weather cools down, it will be time to plant some perennials and a few more overwintering annuals to keep the beds occupied.

Just one little grass weed made it through the paper, leaf mold, lettuce, and nasturtiums.

As Margaret Roach gracefully stated in her seminal work *A Way to Garden*, hers is *a* way, not *the* way to garden, but she hoped it would be helpful for readers. I feel exactly the same with this work. There's no single right way to practice weed-free gardening. Everyone has to find their own balance between accepting certain weeds as ecological necessities and outlawing others as detrimental. Nonetheless, I hope that having a framework for understanding weeds, thinking through the soil work, and considering the carbon concerns we face today will give you new ways to garden for good.

Nature plants multiple layers so soil is protected and carbon is stored year-round.

A New Carboniferous Era

I imagine it's pretty obvious that I have a deep respect for plants others call weeds. But I want to be clear: I see weeds in my landscape as a means to an end. Like you, I want a beautiful garden that reflects my tastes and nurtures me as I nurture it. But I want it long-term, and I know for that to happen we have to act now to solve the climate crisis of the future.

As organic gardeners, we repeatedly hear that the best ways to fight weeds are things like cover our paths with paper and mulch. Mulch around our planting area. Use cover crops. Apply compost.

Don't till. Use closer plant spacing to crowd out weeds. All of these techniques help suppress weeds in the short-term. But for long-term answers, I believe we need to shift our perspective on what it means to grow a garden today.

I think that we are entering a new era, one in which those short-term weed prevention methods will begin to backfire on us. Remember back at the start of the book when we looked at the question of whether early failed farming attempts gave weeds an 11,000-year head start on being ready to grow in agricultural soils? I suggested that instead it was more a case of nature playing the lottery with every number, every time. Well, I also want to posit another theory about our current carbon situation and what it might mean for weeds in the future.

I grow this hairy cat's paw (*Hypochaeris radicata*) in my vineyard on purpose to feed goldfinches and support soil life.

Poke weed (*Hytolacca americana*) is marginally edible for humans but adored and enjoyed by the northern cardinals that live with us on our homestead.

Between about 300 and 350 billion years ago, Earth went through its carboniferous period. Back then, plants were large and abundant, often covered with thick bark as insect protection. The fungi and bacteria we encourage in our soil today hadn't developed the capacity to decompose high lignan plant materials. Much of the plant matter sat on forest floors without decomposing. It was eventually buried under more matter. Of course, down the road, with heat and pressure, that buried carbon-rich material was converted to coal.

As a result of all that carbon being stored, carbon dioxide in the air dropped from about 2,500 parts per million (ppm) to 300 ppm. That decline ultimately made the environment less ideal for plants. Many plant species died out or shrank in size in a lower carbon dioxide atmosphere. Overall, plants became less aggressive in their domination of Earth.

Earth has been through several more periods of big carbon changes due to astronomical and volcanic events. However, every time carbon went high, plants dominated until carbon levels were reduced. Once carbon levels stabilized under 300 ppm, a greater diversity of aboveground non-plant species stepped in to continue cycling carbon back into soil at a more constant rate.

For the roughly 11,000 years since the advent of agriculture until 1850, carbon in the air increased by about 20 ppm. From 1850 to 1950, it went up about 26 ppm to 285 ppm. From 1950 to present, it's increased about 130 ppm to 415 ppm. That now puts us well above the 300 ppm that ended the carboniferous period.

We're living in the range of atmospheric carbon conditions that historically favors plant growth. That should make this a gardener's paradise, right? Unfortunately, the challenge is that, because those increases have happened so quickly, all sorts of other conditions are becoming unstable in response.

Plants that need deer protection grow inside my garden gate. Plants that require less care and nourish wildlife live outside the garden, too.

Weather is more erratic as heat domes, polar vortexes, and El Niño–Southern Oscillation wreak havoc on our daily lives and the health of our gardens. Natural disasters like fires and droughts cause desertification and make environments less suitable for plant growth. Also, invasive plants better suited to changing conditions get in the way of us growing the plants we want to grow. Weeds, as the plants most poised for rapid response given their incredible potential for genetic diversity in just a few generations, are also adapting quickly. They are growing larger, reproducing faster, and adapting to floods and hotter conditions at rates that aren't likely to be matched by cultivated plants anytime soon.

Despite all this, I am not a doomer. I grow a garden in good faith that I'll be able to keep growing it long-term. But I am also a realist. And I know that my ability to maintain my garden depends on whether I embrace the new, more volatile conditions or try to pretend they don't exist.

Weeds have become more aggressive in part because of so many of these factors we've talked about, like monocultures, row spacing, poor soil conditions, and herbicide resistance. But they are also adapting to the new atmospheric carbon realities and our unstable weather conditions. Those conditions clearly favor the success of plants that are able to grow quickly and rapidly reproduce.

I don't think this is about nature playing favorites and giving weeds an advantage. I think nature is trying to reduce atmospheric carbon to make things more favorable for us and other above-ground life-forms, just as what happened throughout Earth's history.

If we want to make peace in our gardens, and invite fewer weeds into them, then we also need to start favoring plants with the most power to successfully store carbon in our gardens. Making peace means accepting that we are gardening in the time of climate change. Yet, this does not have to be bad news. Atmospheric carbon benefits plant growth if we can create the supporting soil habitat to ensure their safety in more volatile growing conditions.

There has never been a better time or a better excuse for you to grow more plants. Plants not only sink carbon, but they also cool the air, shade soil, slow wind, shield from rain, and prevent erosion. They help soil better-absorb moisture after storms and retain it during droughts. They provide habitat for life we can see and life so abundant we will never comprehend its magnitude. And they make our gardens beautiful.

Kiwi, asparagus, horseradish, clary sage, sunflower, chicory, lavender, and lots more plants occupy this small section of my garden.

There's just enough room to step in here and harvest. This plant community of tomato, nasturtium, and zucchini always grows well together in my garden.

This pollinator favorite, purple echinacea (*Echinacea purpurea*), is also a favorite of mine.

References

Bartholomew, Mel. *All New Square Foot Gardening: The Revolutionary Way to Grow More in Less Space.* Beverly, MA: Cool Springs Press, 2013.

Dowding, Charles, and Stephanie Hafferty. *No Dig Organic Home & Garden: Grow, Cook, Use & Store Your Harvest.* East Meon, UK: Permanent Publications, 2017.

Gift, Nancy, and Sheila Rodgers. *Good Weed, Bad Weed: Who's Who, What to Do, and Why Some Deserve a Second Chance (All You Need to Know about the Weeds in Your Yard).* Pittsburgh, PA: St. Lynns Press, 2011.

Hynes, Erin. *Controlling Weeds.* Emmaus, PA: Rodale Press, 1995.

Karsten, Joel. *Straw Bale Gardens Complete: Breakthrough Method for Growing Vegetables Anywhere, Earlier and with No Weeding.* Beverly, MA: Cool Springs Press, 2019.

Mabey, Richard. *Weeds: In Defense of Nature's Most Unloved Plants.* New York: Ecco, 2012.

Muzik, Thomas J. *Weed Biology and Control.* New York: Mcgraw-Hill, 1970.

Nardozzi, Charlie. *The Complete Guide to No-Dig Gardening: Grow Beautiful Vegetables, Herbs, and Flowers—the Easy Way!* Beverly, MA: Cool Springs Press, 2021.

Norris, Kelly D. *New Naturalism: Designing and Planting a Resilient, Ecologically Vibrant Home Garden.* Beverly, MA: Cool Springs Press, 2021.

Reich, Lee. *The Weedless Garden.* New York: Workman, 2001.

Stout, Ruth, and Richard Clemence. *The Ruth Stout No-Work Garden Book: Secrets of the Famous Year-Round Mulch Method.* 16th ed. Emmaus, PA: Rodale Press, 1971.

Thompson, Ken. *The Book of Weeds.* London: DK Publishing, 2009.

Wallington, Jack. *Wild about Weeds: Garden Design with Rebel Plants.* London: Laurence King Publishing, 2019.

Walliser, Jessica. *Plant Partners: Science-Based Companion Planting Strategies to Minimize Disease, Reduce Pests, Improve Soil Fertility, and Support Pollination in the Vegetable Garden.* North Adams, MA: Storey Publishing, 2020.

Zimdahl, Robert L. *Fundamentals of Weed Science.* San Diego, CA: Elsevier, 2018.

About the Author

TASHA GREER

Tasha Greer is an "Epicurean homesteader" and writer focused on simple, sustainable living. She's the author of *Grow Your Own Spices*. Her articles have been posted on *Modern Farmer*, *Mother Earth News*, *The Grow Network*, *Morning Chores*, *House and Homestead*, and *The Thrifty Homesteader*. She teaches classes online and in her community on edible landscaping, composting, growing spices, and organic gardening. You can find her at Simplestead.com.

About the Illustrator

GRETA MOORE

This book was illustrated by Greta Moore, an illustrator and landscape designer in Bozeman, Montana. With an MS in Ecological Landscape Design, she blends her passion for ecology with art to address climate change, improve food systems, restore habitats, create beautiful spaces, and bring plants and animals to life through watercolor paintings. She is also an avid backyard gardener and enjoys adventuring in the mountains and rivers of Montana. To see her work, visit Gretacmoore.com.

Acknowledgments

I have learned from so many researchers, experimenters, and other gardeners that I can't narrow down who to thank for their contributions to this work. Instead, let me give my broad thanks to everyone who digs deeper to understand the minute details that make our gardens grow and shares that information with the rest of us.

I'm also extremely grateful to the Quarto/Cool Springs Press team for their support. Special thanks to my editor (an incredible writer, gardener, and inspiration) Jessica Walliser and the other amazing contributors to this work: Marissa Giambrone, Brooke Pelletier, Steve Roth, Kristine Anderson, Monica Baggio, Katie Benoit Cardoso, Greta Moore, Misilla Dela Llana, Niki Jabbour, Ashlie Thomas, Tim Miles, and others involved behind the scenes.

A huge thanks to my family and community supporters for all the encouragement. I also owe an extra commendation to Matt Miles, my partner in life. He picked up the slack around our homestead and gave me the support I needed to go deep into the weeds and create a work that will help gardeners navigate new environmental pressures.

Finally, to all you gardeners out there, you have my deep appreciation for the work you do to collaborate with nature and grow a more ecologically beautiful world. Keep learning, experimenting, and sharing your love with others!

Index

Jerusalem artichokes (*Helianthus tuberosus*), 59, *59*

jewelweed (*Impatiens capensis*), 58

Jimsonweed (*Datura stramonium*), 60, 125, *125*

Job's tears (*Coix lacryma-jobi*), 6

journals, 77, *77*

K

Karsten, Joel, 148–149

kudzu (*Pueraria montana*), 56

L

lambsquarters (*Chenopodium album*), 40, *40*

landscape
  drainage and, 92–98
  edible, 145
  getting to know, 75–76

landscapes, weeds entering, 24–37

lasagna gardening, 69–70, 158–159

Latin names, use of, 44

lava rock, 165

layered bed-making, 158–159

layered planting, 68

layout, 76

leaf mold, 102

leaves, 156

legal codes, 75

lespedeza (*Kummerowia striata*, syn. *Lespedeza striata*), 60

life cycle disruption, 42

lignite, 111

lilac (*Syringa vulgaris*), 58

living mulch, 32

locusts, 79

longevity, 46

low-till gardening, 122–123

lupine (*Lupinus* spp.), 47

M

machine tillers, 88

maintenance
  drainage, 85–98
  introduction to, 81–83
  mycorrhizal networks, 112–113
  organic matter, 99–111
  soil, 83–85

manual tillers, 88

maypop (*Passiflora incarnata*), 6, 137

mint, 11, 110

mistletoes (*Phoradendron leucarpum*), 67

moisture, excess, 46. *See also* water

Mollison, Bill, 21

monoculture, 73

mops, 60

mounds, 98

mowing, 128–130

mugwort (*Artemisia vulgaris*), 7, 137

mulch
  adding organic matter with, 101–105
  bamboo, 134
  as best prevention, 17
  brown leaf, 102–103
  choosing, *82*, 110–111
  high-carbon, 101, 103
  high-nitrogen, 104–105, 110
  living, 32
  natural, 9
  needle, 102–103
  no-work gardening method and, 153
  as preemptive measure, 25–26
  rock, 164–166
  sand-based soil and, 92
  sheet mulching, 158–159
  trial beds for, *101*
  wood mulch gardening, 157–158
  wood-based, 102

mushroom compost, 25–26

    WEED-FREE GARDENING

rock beds, 47

rock dust, 166

rock mulches, 164–166

root structures, 52–60

root washing, 27, *27*

Rose, Stephania, 76

round point shovels, 39

Ruth Stout No-Work Garden Book, The (Stout and Clemence), 153

S

sand-based soil, 90–92

scythes, 129, *129*

seasonality, 68–72

seeds

    auto-germinating, 40

    dormancy and, 40

    inspection of, *36*

    starting in cells, 37

    weed seeds in, 35–37

shade, as control measure, 71, *159*

sheet mulching, 158–159

sickles, 129, *129*

slime mold (*Fuligo septica*), 158

slow pile compost method, 100

smartweed (*Persicaria pensylvanica*, syn. *Polygonum pensylvanicum*), 71, *71*

soaker hoses, 62, *62*

sodium bicarbonate, 82, 83

soil

    acidic, 45

    alkaline, 46

    clay heavy, 86–87, *87*

    description of, 83–85

    drainage and, 85–98

    dry, 46

    humic content of, 111

sand-based, 90–92

soil aerators, 87–88, *88*

soil amendments, 29, 31, 32–33

soil disturbance

    as entry point, 45

        post-disturbance protection, 26

        seed germination and, 25

soil preparation, 38

soil qualities, 45

soil type, 76

solarizing, 124, *124*

Sonora wheat, *149*

sow thistle (*Sonchus oleraceus*), 77

Spanish moss (*Tillandsia usneoides*), 66

speedwell (*Veronica* spp), 60

spiny amaranth (*Amaranthus spinosus*), 10, *10*, 16

spotted lanternfly, 12

square foot gardening, 146–148

stable carbon, 86

stake test, 33

stinging nettle (*Urtica dioica*), 40, *40–41*, 110

stirrup hoe, 30, *30*

Stout, Ruth, 153

straight row cropping, 14

straw bale gardening, 148–153, *152, 172–173*

Straw Bale Gardens Complete (Karsten), 148–149

strawberries, 11, *162*

string trimmers, 130, *130*

swales, 98

synthetic nitrogen fertilizer, 117

T

taproots

    branching, 54–55, *54*

    deep, 52–54, *52–53*

    storage, 55

tarps, 32

teosinte, 18–19

thatching, 72

thermophilic compost piles, 69–70, 100, *100*

Thomas, Ashlie, 139–140